# MILLENNIAL MOMS

**202** FACTS MARKETERS NEED TO KNOW TO BUILD BRANDS AND DRIVE SALES

## Maria T. Bailey

Wyatt-MacKenzie Publishing
DEADWOOD, OREGON

# DEDICATION

To my children, Madison, Owen, Keenan and Morgan,
who motivate me to always go above and beyond.

Millennial Moms: 202 Facts Marketers Need to Know
to Build Brands and Drive Sales
Maria T. Bailey

ISBN: 978-1-939288-91-2
Library of Congress Control Number: 2015946498

Edited by Lisa Pliscou
Proofread by Karen Kibler
Indexed by Jean Jesensky, Ends Well Indexing
Book design and graphics by Shauna Lewis, BSM Media

Wyatt-MacKenzie Publishing
DEADWOOD, OREGON

Wyatt-MacKenzie Publishing, Inc.
www.WyattMacKenzie.com

# CONTENTS

# INTRODUCTION

Millennial Moms. There's probably no topic that's more currently discussed in the Mom Market. The buzz is rightly earned. No generation of mothers presents so much opportunity for brands — and this certainty comes from a person who's written about every cohort since the Baby Boomers. Wow, just writing that makes me feel old! As I sat down to write this book I couldn't help but reminisce about the evolution of Mom Marketing and my journey through it. When I wrote *Marketing to Moms: Getting Your Share of the Trillion-Dollar Market* in 2002, I was a Boomer Mom with four young children; I didn't understand why companies cared about the money I was spending on their products. The book got modest attention but most marketing professionals dismissed the topic of marketing to moms because they felt their current women-targeted initiatives were doing the job.

Then in 2005 I wrote *Trillion-Dollar Moms: Marketing to a New Generation of Mothers* in order to examine a unique time in history when multiple generations of mothers were having babies all at once. We learned as marketers that the age of a mom's child was more important than her own age in determining her values and behaviors. The influence of technology hit the Mom Market hard in the mid-00s and I saw a need to write *Mom 3.0: Marketing with Today's Mothers by Leveraging New Media & Technology*. Just as I had to make a last-minute edit on this book to add in Periscope, the newest social media platform to be catching fire in the Mom Market, I remembered to go back to *Mom 3.0* and add in Twitter. It was a time when

Mom Bloggers were believed to be the silver bullet of Mom Marketing and MySpace and Facebook were the discussions of the day. Mom Bloggers gained influence by broadening their reach not only online through Twitter and Facebook, but offline as well as they booked television segments and hosted social media conferences in their hometowns. I named these highly influential moms "Power Moms," and titled my eighth book with the same name. The Millennials were beginning to make their mark among the social media–savvy Generation Xers about this time and it became clear to me that it was time to start writing again.

The book you are reading on an e-reader, listening to on a device or holding in your hands has been in the works for over three years. It's taken me longer than any other book to compile for a number of reasons, the greatest being the rapid change that has occurred in this massive generation. Just about the time I felt we were getting to know the Millennial Moms born around 1980, the younger Millennials began influencing the Mom Market. Advances in technology added to the dynamic nature of the Millennial generation as well. I finally decided to draw a line in the sand and publish *Millennial Moms* before it was time to write about the Post Generation — those tweens and teens who will be the next generation of mothers.

The decision to write a book about a selected topic is the easiest part of the process. You may expect me to say that the most challenging is the hours of research or analysis or typing over 60,000 words, but neither earns the top spot in difficulty. The most challenging part is choosing the style and format of the book. No one wants to read 100 pages of straight research. Long chapters of opinion and case studies aren't the recipe for success either. When I approached this book, I had three goals.

First, to provide marketers with a fast read on Millennial Moms that would enable them to execute strategies quickly and successfully. Second, provide insights that were deeper and more relevant than marketing professionals could find anywhere else. If I have read once, I've read it a hundred times: "Moms are busy and using technology in their hectic lives." Let's all agree now that we know moms are busy and are using technology in their hectic lives! What I wanted to provide brand professionals is the insight into *what* technology specifically and *how* marketing managers can insert their product, brand or company into that behavior to make money.

That's why we're in this game, isn't it? To make money? I know that my business school professors have drilled that simple statement into my mind. I want to give marketers the tools to make money in the Millennial Mom Market but I want to do it — and here comes number three — without putting my reader to sleep. That's quite a challenge in a world of 140-character tweets and a six-second Vine tutorial, and it required a special format to achieve all three. Fortunately, I didn't have to go further than my subject matter to find what I believe is the perfect format. I took my cues from Millennial Moms who consume content in quick, short "sound-bytes." Sometimes the content is condensed to an image on Instagram or 140 characters on Twitter — so that's exactly what you'll find in *Millennial Moms*.

My team at BSM Media and I dug through thousands of pages of research and data to find 202 of the most relevant facts about Millennial Moms. We created infographics that communicate our points in images, much like a Millennial does on Pinterest, Tumblr or Facebook. Interesting facts are called out in 140 characters or less so that you can easily share them with others on Twitter. We even included the hashtag #Millennial-Moms for you. Walking in the shoes of your customer is a "Marketing 101" lesson, so we figured you'd benefit from consuming this content in much the same way as the consumer we're trying to reach — Millennial Moms.

Now, I will confess that it wasn't easy to streamline all the knowledge, insights and commentary I wanted to include so that it would fit into the desired format. In fact, you'll find some of the long paragraphs that many of us are used to seeing in textbooks. I didn't want to rob my audience of the many resources I can deliver in this book or the ample experience my team at BSM Media has had in successfully connecting with Millennial Moms on behalf of our clients. I will make this offer several times in the coming pages. If there is subject matter or a fact you find particularly relevant to your business and you find yourself saying, "I wish Maria had written more about this," please act like a Millennial and text me at +1 (954) 261-2145 or tweet me @MomTalkRadio. If you want to act like a Baby Boomer or Gen Xer, I will happily answer my phone when you call or reply to the email you send to maria@bsmmedia.com. My point is that I love talking about Mom Marketing and am always open to sharing my passion with you. You don't have to be a client. Please contact me with questions. Chances are we have more information on the subjects you need to know.

Regarding the content of *Millennial Moms*, you'll find a combination of research, case studies, anecdotes and quotes from actual members of the Millennial generation. Let me speak to the research. There are many organizations in our industry doing qualitative and quantitative research — Pew Research Center and BabyCenter.com to mention two. Some of the research is not specifically targeted to Millennials with children but there are nuggets that are applicable to the Millennial Mom. We noted insights and research from third-party groups when we thought it would provide value to the book. In addition, BSM Media conducted its own research about Millennial Moms. For over 20 years, my company has been tracking the behavior of mothers not only for my books but also for clients. There are some insights from years of historical data as well as current trends and analysis as part of our ongoing research.

For *Millennial Moms*, we launched the largest research project in two decades. We surveyed over 3,000 moms of all generations with an equal number of Boomers, Gen Xers and Millennials. Additionally, we conducted focus groups, social listening and kitchen-counter conversations: our version of informal discussions. The project produced over 300 pages of data that we ultimately segmented in a myriad of ways from generational to geographical. We also pulled together any research that we've conducted in the last year for clients who gave us permission to share in *Millennial Moms*. As a Boomer who prefers to read from printed pages, I can say with confidence that there are over 1,000 pages of research behind this book. The best part is that it's been crunched, analyzed and reformatted down to the pages you have before you. As discussed above, some have even been condensed to a 100-plus character tweet because I know that like moms, you are busy. I am confident that you'll find a surplus of data — so much so that I decided to balance it out with interviews with real live Millennial Moms. No one conveys an insight better than an actual consumer so we enlisted some to provide their opinions. It was the suggestion of ElizaBeth Fincannon on my team that we include the mom's age next to her quote. ElizaBeth thought it would be a great way to note whether the mom is an older or younger Millennial and I agreed, so you'll see this information displayed. I've hinted that there is a difference in behaviors among Millennials and I'll address this later in the introduction. In conducting interviews, I did come across a few insights that were very interesting albeit from a Generation Xer. I included and noted them. After all, even though the focus of Millennial Moms is women born between 1980 and 2000, updating what we know about Gen Xers and Boomers is also relevant to capturing today's Mom Market. You'll find that we used generational comparisons throughout the book in order to help you freshen up on your knowledge of all three cohorts of mothers.

While I'm talking about generations, I would like to address the unique division of the Millennial era.

Technology has been the greatest driver of behavioral characteristics for this group — so much so that it's created a divide between older Millennials and younger Millennials. The older Millennial Moms, defined as ages 27 – 35, were introduced to technology during their elementary school years. Their families likely had a large PC and heavy monitor in a shared area of the home. AOL told them they had mail and their parents had parental-control software installed. At school the library became a "media center" with a computer lab. They learned technology as it evolved. In contrast, younger Millennials were born into technology. They never knew a time when a laptop wasn't present and email wasn't a mainstream form of communication. Today some of these girls/women are still in high school where socializing largely takes place on their smartphone. As technology has evolved it has impacted the behaviors of the youngest Millennials in ways that are innate rather than learned as with the older

Millennials. For this reason, I will call out differences where they exist with the cohort and compare behaviors where it is appropriate.

I think research and insights are important but only as useful as knowing how to apply it to create results for your company. For that reason, you'll find a section called "Marketing Implications" following many of the 202 Millennial Mom Facts. Here I provided ideas for your company to apply the data to actual tactics. Some will be based on programs BSM Media has developed that produce successful results in the Mom Market. I don't mind if you borrow them. In fact, I encourage you to do so. The goal of this book is to empower you to tap the Millennial Mom Market and your success is my success. Again, I offer my help if you have additional questions about any of the Marketing Implications. You can email me at maria@bsmmedia.com.

This is an exciting time to be marketing to moms. Millennial Moms bring a new influx of consumer behaviors and values. They are willing to try new products, are wise shoppers and love to share information with friends and families. While the total Millennial generation numbers vary between 80–83 million people in the U.S., only an estimated one-third of Millennial women have become mothers. The time is right to get ready for what's to come. With 202 Facts, you should be prepared to tap into the very lucrative market represented by this young generation of mothers.

Let's get started.

# CHAPTER
# 1

# Millennials:
# The General Facts

**#1** **Millennial Moms will spend approximately $750 billion a year.**

**#2** **2015 is the year that Millennials become the largest generation of consumers.**

**#3** **The Millennial generation is the largest cohort since the Baby Boomers. According to the latest U.S. Census Bureau report[1], there are 83.1 million Millennials.**

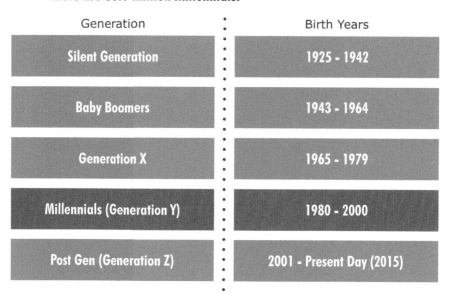

| Generation | Birth Years |
|---|---|
| Silent Generation | 1925 - 1942 |
| Baby Boomers | 1943 - 1964 |
| Generation X | 1965 - 1979 |
| Millennials (Generation Y) | 1980 - 2000 |
| Post Gen (Generation Z) | 2001 - Present Day (2015) |

**#4** **There are currently an estimated 13 million Millennial moms in the U.S., only about one-third of the 42 million Millennial women in the U.S.**

**#5** **Millennial Moms will spend approximately $750 billion a year.**

U.S. mothers spend approximately $2.3 trillion dollars a year in the U.S. economy. It's a number that is thrown around in nearly every article written about marketing to mothers, many times without proper accreditation. In 1999, after hours of number-crunching and searching government data, I calculated the annual spending of U.S. moms for my first book, *Marketing to Moms: Getting Your Piece of the Trillion-Dollar Market* (Prima, 2002). Every year since then, my team and I recalculate this number. It's with great excitement that we break out the current spending of Millennial Moms. I expect that this number will continue to grow as the population of Millennial females transitions into motherhood.

Remember, the youngest Millennials are still teenagers and they are delaying the age at which they have their first child, so it could be another decade before we experience the full impact of the spending power of Millennial Moms. It's important to be ready.

## #6 She is the daughter of a Baby Boomer or a Gen Xer and "You're special" was the mantra of her childhood.

As children, Millennial Moms were told over and over again that they were special and now as adults they expect the world to treat them as such.

### #TakeNote

What does this mean to marketers? You have to up your game on customer service and product offerings with exclusive items and loyalty programs that recognize these traits and allow them to feel, yes, special.

## #7 Millennials are postponing marriage.

Marriage, seen for generations as a milestone to adulthood and responsibility, has taken a backseat for Millennials. Looking at the numbers, the marriage rate has declined by about 50% since the 1960s.[2] More recent numbers show that the marriage rate has decreased by 10.3 marriages per 1,000 unmarried women (ages 15 and older) from 2001 to 2011.[3] The median age of first-time marriages for women has increased to age 27, the oldest age yet, while the average age for men to get married for the first time is 29.[4]

Children born to unmarried parents jumped from 12% in 2002 to 24% in 2010,[5] supporting a Pew Research Study showing a 26% marriage rate among Millennials in 2014. As stated in the same study, when they were at the same age as Millennials are now, 36% of Generation X, 48% of Baby Boomers and 65% of the Silent Generation were married. The logical reason for this decline might be that it's in line with the Millennials' distrust of conventional institutions. However, I would argue that it's a combination of several factors.

First, a higher percentage of Millennial women are getting advanced degrees, which could mean they're putting off marriage until they complete their education. Second, they watched their parents deal with balancing work and family and are hesitant to reenact that lifestyle until they're financially ready. Finally, many Millennials are moving back home after college, with more debt than prior generations. Living at home, eating Mom's dinners and focusing on paying off college loans doesn't leave much extra time or attention for finding a mate. In the next few pages, you'll learn that Millennials are pragmatic. They do things when it makes sense to them. One could argue that it doesn't make sense to get married at age 22, possibly unemployed and living at home.

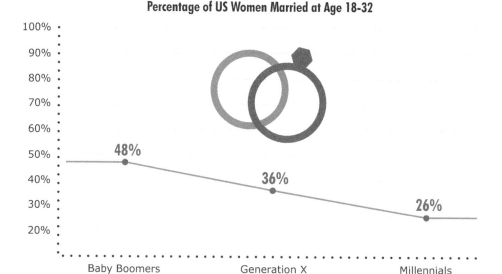

**Percentage of US Women Married at Age 18-32**

# #8 "Happy" trumps "politically correct" when it comes to marriage.

Ashton Kutcher and Mila Kunis. Kourtney Kardashian and Scott Disick. Shakira and Gerard Pique. These are just a few examples from pop culture of the growing number of non-married with children along; I refer you back to the reasons listed in Fact #7. The pursuit of happiness is more important to this generation than conforming to a group of standards or social norms. The Millennials have demonstrated their acceptance of diversity and the unique values that individuals bring to life. They have embraced same-sex marriages; multicultural relationships are no longer considered unusual. For this group of parents, whatever makes you and your family happy is more important than a license that says you're married.

## #TakeNote

Understanding the values around marriage for your target market and visualizing images of marriage are important aspects of marketing to any generation. The use of June Cleaver was effective in marketing to older Boomers while images of Marge Simpson connected with Generation X mothers. To effectively connect with Millennial Moms, brands need to use images of families that support their acceptance of diversity and marriage. Cheerios hit a home run with their use of a racially blended marriage in a commercial that aired in 2013. Although it caused many Boomer parents to take a second, slightly shocked look, it was well received by Millennial Moms. What's popular on TV presents valuable insights regarding the images that connect with Millennial Moms. Shows such as *Modern Family* put the spotlight on multicultural and same-sex marriages that are in line with the views of Millennial Moms. As a marketer, you may need to look beyond your own values or those of consumers around you and say, "I understand you" in a way that speaks to your target market.

#MillennialMoms prefer inclusive marketing campaigns that feature varieties of families not represented in their parents' generation.

## #9 Historically, there are more single moms than ever.

Even though Millennial Moms are delaying the age when they first get married, that's not stopping them from becoming mothers. In 2012, 21% of births to women over 34 were out of wedlock, compared to 47% of those born to unmarried Millennial women.[6] What is interesting is that the population of single Millennial Moms is growing while the rate of teen pregnancies is declining, according to a report by the Department of Health and Human Services. The rate of teen pregnancy, which includes the very youngest Millennials, declined by 10% between 2012 and 2013.[7] This would indicate that Millennial Moms are single by choice and entering parenthood at an age later than their teens.

I wrote a great deal about single-by-choice mothers in *Trillion-Dollar Moms: Marketing to a New Generation of Mothers (Kaplan Business, 2005)* because it was such a new trend with the emergence of the Generation X mother. However, data from the National Center for Health Statistics indicates that Millennial Moms are taking the trend to new highs. When Gen Xer moms were the same age as Millennial Moms are today, only 35% of births were out of wedlock compared to the 47% of Millennial out-of-wedlock births today. It's likely that the value these Millennial females put on children has impacted the increase in single mothers.

## #10 There is a renewed value placed on children.

Prior to the Industrial Revolution, families valued children as added help in the fields or around the house. Baby Boomers held their children up as status symbols. No matter the value of children historically, the Millennial parent has redefined the value of children today. Millennial Moms have placed a heightened value on children. To understand the evolution of this value, we must again examine the childhood of a Millennial

Mom. The birth of the first successful "test tube baby" in the United States took place in 1978, just two years before the official start of the Millennial generation. With media attention put on test tube babies, known more appropriately as babies born via in vitro fertilization (IVF), couples in the 80s and 90s clamored to get into fertility clinics. It took months to get an appointment and couples laid down large sums of money to conceive children. As teenagers, the oldest Millennials watched on television as new parents celebrated the birth of twins, triplets and quadruplets, which were almost always conceived via fertility procedures. Magazines and TV specials brought attention to the growing trend of surrogate mothers and Millennials watched as stars like Brad Pitt and Angelina Jolie adopted children from foreign countries. The world told the Millennials that children were valuable and a gift that brought joy to one's life.

*"I always knew I wanted to be a mom, but I wasn't in a big hurry to start motherhood. I wanted to finish all of my education first and have some time with my husband. (I also always knew I'd adopt my kids.) We adopted our first child when I was 27 and he was 35, after we were married for almost eight years. We'd have waited a bit longer, but based on his age we were concerned about him reaching the upper limits that some countries have in place for adoptive parents. It worked out perfectly for us."—Laura W., 35*

*"I never intended to have children. I intended to have a professional career, possibly a husband one day. After marriage, motherhood just sort of happened. In fact, motherhood 'happened' a second, third and even fourth time in my life. Until becoming a mother, I never knew life could be so chaotically wonderful. Having children brought me more laughter, joy and memories than I ever knew possible. It has helped me understand the world more, have more compassion and patience, and discover a new person in myself that I didn't know existed before having these children. The best part has been discovering that motherhood encompasses professionalism, education, career, fitness, and family. It all looks different than I thought it would but it's so much better than I intended."—Alice C., 36*

# #11 Diversity abounds.

It has been widely documented that the Millennial generation is the most diverse population in the history of our country. According to U.S. Census data, the makeup of this generation is 61% white, 19% Hispanic, 14% African-American, 5% Asian and 1% other. By 2020, the most common last name is likely to be "Rodriguez" as predicted by the bureau. Millennials only know a world where multiculturalism exists and best friends may be from countries on the other side of the world.

## #TakeNote

Millennials may not understand your desire to segment your marketing messages. For marketers who are still creating marketing strategies that separate messages for, say, the Hispanic and African-American communities, this may be an outdated approach for Millennials. They don't understand why anyone would speak to one group differently than another. In the minds of Millennials, who accept everyone for who they are, this seems like a very antiquated approach. Now I know there are some marketers who have a pile of research on their desk telling them otherwise. Data that says one cultural group acts differently than the other is easily found in books and in nicely bound reports from research companies. I am not disagreeing with the numbers you might read. I'm merely speaking from the perspective of Millennials who do not see the "segments" around people which some research may indicate. It can be confusing. You may choose to do things the way you've already done them and get decent, even good results; however, I encourage you to look at the world through the lens of a Millennial. I predict that by 2020 many marketing budgets devoted solely to one ethnic group will be gone.

# #12 They are optimistic about the future.

In our survey, 74% of Millennial Moms feel optimistic about the future. Another 44% feel that the future offers a better world than the one experienced by their parents. The optimistic view on life may originate in the Millennials' self-confidence and the historical events they've witnessed. The events of 9/11 demonstrated to them that human kindness and compassion could rise from hate and tragedy. The 2007 recession gave them the opportunity to be creative and find new ways to stretch their dollar and emerge as better individuals. Millennials are not only optimistic for the future, but Baby Boomers and Generation Xers place their hope for a better world on Millennials' shoulders as well.

 **74%** of Millennial Moms reported feeling optimistic about the future

*"Millennials are optimistic about the future because we have the power to create, change and recreate our circumstances. I feel that as Millennials we are more in touch with what we need to be successful and enrich our lives. With that ability comes responsibilities and opportunities. I think we have a stronger sense of self, and have no problem expressing that 'we got this.'"—Jennifer G., 33*

## #13 Millennial Moms have a desire to serve others.

Two decades ago, cultural predictions centered on Millennials being the generation that saved the rest of us. They were teenagers and the world watched as they raised millions of dollars in relief funds for tsunami victims in Indonesia and then donated their time during spring break to clean up damage from Hurricane Katrina. They were the first generation required to perform volunteer hours in order to graduate from high school.

However, it didn't require strict academic policies to motivate this generation to give back. They were motivated by the desire to achieve greatness. Their parents instilled in them the idea that they were capable of doing anything and that their talents could change the world, and they believed it. So while other generations submitted grades and essays on their college applications, the Millennials attached news articles and background papers for fundraising or not-for-profit organizations they created as teenagers. Millennial Moms most likely donated birthday presents to charity, collected items as part of a clothing, food or toy drive or shared after-school hours with less fortunate children. This generation has a heart for serving and the ambition to do so on a grand scale.

## #TakeNote

Cause marketing is an effective way to connect a brand and Millennial Moms. We'll discuss this topic at greater length later in this book.

## #14 Millennials define their generation by technology.

Many professionals in marketing, research, media and academia have defined Millennials. We decided to go directly to the source to get their opinions on the broad issues they feel define their generation. Technology, pop culture and social issues such as poverty and crime were the most popular answers. Although Gen X moms defined their generation similarly, the Millennials put a greater importance on these subjects as well as on education.

**Issues Millennial Moms Believe Define Their Generation**

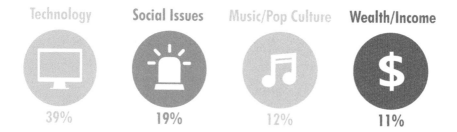

| Technology | Social Issues | Music/Pop Culture | Wealth/Income |
| --- | --- | --- | --- |
| 39% | 19% | 12% | 11% |

Source: BSM Media, 2015

## #15 She is networked and connected.

At a rate of 86%, the Millennial Moms we surveyed claim to carry at least two wireless devices on a regular basis, with the majority toting around four to five devices. The largest group of Gen Xer moms surveyed carries two or three devices. Over 10% described themselves as regularly carrying five or more wireless gadgets. All of this technology in her purse, stroller or diaper bag makes it easy to hop on the Internet and might explain how these Millennial Moms report a daily average of four hours online. A full 11% of our Millennials told us that they're on their wireless device(s) for more than seven hours each day. You might be wondering, "Who are these women talking to?" We asked them.

At least 42% say they have more than 500 friends on their personal Facebook page. That's a lot of people and status updates each day, and it's not just Facebook occupying online time. Instagram, Twitter and Pinterest are the most popular social media platforms, with YouTube and LinkedIn bringing up the rear. Over 35% of our moms surveyed said they speak to more than 21 moms either online or in person each week. Online, they belong to an average of six groups and offline — an area of influence marketers often forget — 56% of our Millennial Moms belong to up to three groups. She's connected and uses technology to share, socialize and shop; chances are she's checked her smartphone at least once in the last hour.

## #16 She wants it *now* and she wants it fast.

Call her impatient, but the Millennial Mom doesn't like to wait. Why should she? She's had information at her fingertips since she was young. She has developed skills that allow her to search for the resources she needs when she needs them. She might not wear a watch but she is acutely attuned to time. Whether she's searching your website for product specifications or purchasing an item from your app, the Millennial Mom expects a fast and easy experience.

We gave our moms a list of everyday situations and asked them to note the amount of time they were willing to wait for each before giving up and moving on. Millennial Moms give up sooner than Gen X and Boomer mothers in every single situation. The former is willing to wait up to 10 minutes for a cup of coffee but when it comes to technology, it'd better be fast. Almost 42% of Millennials will give up on a website to load if it doesn't happen in less than one minute. When it comes to apps, the number grows. If an app takes longer than one minute to load on her wireless device, 44% say they will move on. This doesn't give brands much time to win her over, so it's important to move quickly.

If you are a brand that wants her to subscribe to a newsletter, beware. The most time she will devote to your cause is two minutes. These women are a bit more patient with text messages, however. Over 50% of Millennial Moms said they would wait more than 10 minutes for a reply to a text before giving up on a response.

Speed is an interesting concept with moms of all generations. It's one that isn't unique to the Millennial. It's been documented over and over again that moms are busy. In fact, every time I read that statement in a research report, I cringe. We all know this and yet marketers still do not take this simple fact into consideration when creating apps, launching campaigns or communicating with their mom customers. Here's an example that I'll bet happens every day in Michaels or Jo-Ann Fabric and Craft stores. Standing in the checkout line, a mom realizes she forgot her coupon at home. She goes online to pull one off the store's website. She must navigate no fewer than four pages to reach the coupon for her purchase. Now let's step back for a minute and look at this customer execution from the marketer's side.

The coupon was probably meant to drive her into the store. Or if she's in the store already, to drive her to purchase incremental items. However, I've been on the marketing side long enough to know that a CRM person probably saw the coupon program, then jumped in and asked to collect her information while she was receiving the coupon. The merchandising department asked to push out product information to her before she got the coupon. The IT department then told the brand manager that there was only one way to do it. And before you know it, the coupon is buried far below all these secondary strategies and lost to the customer who wanted to use the coupon for incremental purchases. Almost 40% of our Millennial Moms said they would invest only one minute to the process of downloading a coupon. By the way, 42% of them will only stand in that retail line for up to five minutes before they are headed out the door. Moms want it when they need it and when they need it is now. It's that simple. Millennial Moms buy and shop solutions, so if you want to be her source for solutions, you have to operate at her speed.

**Maximum Time Millennial Moms Will Invest with Brands**

Video to Load . . . . . . . . . . . . . . . < 90 seconds

Online Check Out . . . . . . . . . . . . . 4 minutes

On Phone with Customer Service . . . . 10 minutes

Drive Thru Line . . . . . . . . . . . . . . . 4 minutes

# #17 Millennials want instant gratification.

You may wonder why I didn't include instant gratification with speed. After all, at first glance they might seem one and the same. Instant gratification for the Millennial Moms goes deeper than speed. Instant gratification is an emotional quality while speed is a reactionary quality. Recall how the Millennials received praise for almost every action and effort they put forth as a child. Video games such as Club Penguin and Webkinz gave the youngest Millennials points for their actions. As adults, those Millennials expect and desire the same real-time reaction from the people, companies and technology they interact with each day. On Facebook, they enjoy getting "likes" and if a photo posted on Instagram receives little to no interaction, they may remove it. Instant gratification is a standard for acceptance. For younger Millennials in particular, it's a way they communicate with friends via social media. It reconfirms their popularity among their peers, publicly demonstrates acceptance of other individuals' unique qualities and gives them a way to express their opinions. However, not all "likes" are equal. I'll talk in much more detail about "likes" in the chapter on brands later in the book.

I think it's important to highlight the impact of instant gratification for the younger Millennial. The use of "likes" and comments has shaped the confidence level of younger Millennials as much as the approval of their parents. Many of these younger cohorts post selfies in large quantities, with the intent to gain peer response. A lack of "likes" can be demoralizing. It's almost as if a generation of teenagers has based their self-confidence on the number of "likes" they receive on their photos. This type of posting also opens the doors to cyber-bullying, which also impacts their measure of self-worth. I bring this behavior to your attention because I expect that it will be one that defines the younger Millennial crowd as they enter their 30s over the next decade. As a marketer, it's always good to know what's coming and for young Millennials, I see a group of consumers who will need constant validation and a lot of attention.

 #MillennialMoms love to be "liked" on social media. Including this kind of engagement in your social strategy is imperative.

Music and photos are two areas that illustrate the value Millennials put on instant gratification. Let's look at how music has changed for all generations. For the Baby Boomers it was all about the vinyl. A teenager saved her money and went to the store and bought her favorite music album. It got easier for the Gen Xer who collected tapes and CDs and if she wanted to hear a song, she could insert the disc and listen. She could take her music with her on a Sony Walkman. Then came the iPod. Suddenly a music lover could hear whatever song she wanted, whenever she wanted it, as long as she had her iPod updated. For Millennials, music is instantaneous. She can listen to, and in some cases watch, the music she wants in a few quick swipes, taps or clicks. The Millennial can pick up her mood with Pharrell Williams's song "Happy" or get romantic with Beyoncé's "Drunk in Love" on her iPad, iPod, smartphone, laptop or smart appliances.

Music can be accessed anytime and sets the standard for other technology applications for the Millennial Mom. Photos join music in the category of trendsetters. Who could have imagined, in the days we took film to the local drugstore and then waited three days for prints, that the majority of Americans would carry a camera with them on a daily basis in the form of a phone?

Photography has become an instant hobby for every selfie-loving, Instagram-crazed Millennial. For most of the younger Millennials, it's the only kind of photography they have ever known. It's almost humorous to those of us of a certain age that Polaroid cameras are now a vintage item in high demand on eBay. Photography has contributed to the instant-gratification standard that Millennials demand from all technology and most products they purchase. They wanted a quick way to edit their smartphone photos so app creators gave them Instagram. They wanted an easy way to edit video clips together so developers created Vine. Instant gratification comes in many forms, from feeling proud of a photo to experiencing the sense of accomplishment when you send a customized gift to a friend.

Across all categories, quick resolution is another form of immediate gratification that Millennials want from a company. Marketers often forget customer service when it comes to marketing to moms. However, it's one of the most important elements of connecting with the market. Whether it's an online chat or an easy-to-find 1-800 number, Millennial Moms are more likely to purchase from a brand they know delivers quick customer service. It's time to catch up to Millennials because they are moving fast.

## #18 Customization is a way of life.

Millennial Moms were raised on customization. Since the time they were children, they have been customizing products. From their teddy bears at Build-A-Bear Workshop to their coffee at Starbucks, customization is the norm for Millennial Moms. They expect that your brand will provide a way for them to customize the product to their lifestyle whether it's in color, packaging or delivery options. Customization affirms to the Millennial that you recognize her ability to make and create choices that best fit her family's needs and that she is special in her own unique way.

There are several brands leveraging the Millennial Mom's desire to customize products. In the category of technology, Apple leads the way, from the days when consumers could select color, size and storage capacity for iPods. Today, they are promising to push the envelope with the Apple watch that is launching with 10 different watch faces but rumors say there will be over 200 choices. Millennial women can customize jewelry collections such as Origami Owl, one of the hottest new brands among Millennials and the Post Generation. This jewelry line allows you to select charms that are inserted into necklaces or bracelets. Customization is no longer considered an added value for Millennials. It's a point of entry when developing products for this generation.

## #19 The Millennial Mom exudes confidence.

The Millennial Mom feels confident in everything she does, from raising children to running a business. After all, her parents convinced her that she could do anything and technology has enabled her to achieve whatever she desires. The confidence of the Millennial Mom can also be seen in her willingness to take risks. We see this unique quality every day on Pinterest and Instagram where she posts her attempts at new recipes, craft projects and home improvement. This is a welcome trait for marketers with new products. Millennial Moms are open to trying new flavors, experimenting with products and testing services that might help them in their busy lives.

Many members of the older generations have accused the Millennial generation of being overly assertive, but older generations may be confusing the overconfidence of this cohort with being pushy. The same Baby Boomers who like to gripe that Millennials have strong opinions are the generation that instilled in their younger cohort this high level of confidence. In a discussion with a group of Millennials about becoming a

new mom, one woman put it in these words: "I'
know more than our mothers did about parent'
we are better prepared for motherhood." A '
might take a Boomer aback a bit but, as she ˙.
technology allows her and her friends to research ᴄ.
of a new baby before the baby arrives.

## #TakeNote

Acknowledge her desire to exhibit her confidence by allow-ing her to leave feedback, recommend product changes and share her thoughts with others. Brands should also never speak down to her. She may be a beginner but she exhibits the confidence of a professional and you have to treat her as such.

*"As a busy working mother I am always ready to try new products that make my life easier. I do find using social media a place to go to find new and healthy recipes. I have found that being less uptight and more adventurous allows both myself and my children to feel more empowered. Living in this 'information age' gives me the chance to try things I normally wouldn't. As far as taking risks, I think it is extremely important for both myself and my children to step outside our comfort zone. It gives my children an invaluable lesson when they try something new and it starts to click. Maybe this was something that before they were very reluctant to try. But if you just keep trying and trying it teaches my children the rewards of hard work."—Colleen S., 31*

*"I think I am a total risk taker, but with knowledge everything has consequences. I will try anything once. I am going back to school at age 35 and while I'm nervous being the sole provider for my kids, I know it will provide us a better life."—Karon R., 35*

*"For me, both of my parents worked. I grew up coming home alone (with my brother) from school, and seeing my parents work hard for all that we had. I was mature and self- sufficient at a young age and know what it means to have a full time job. I personally am not afraid of failure. I was allowed to explore a lot as a child (creatively and actively) and made a lot of mistakes along the way. I understand that it's all part of the process."—Allison W., 31*

## Transparency is a must for the Millennial Mom.

Transparency is important to Millennial Moms because it's a reflection of what it represents: established relationships and a sense of security. Over 50% of Millennial Moms in the BSM Media survey say that transparency is "extremely important" when selecting a brand or product while 35% think it is "somewhat important."

The flip side for established and mom-trusted brands is the dreaded recall. Witness the string of Children's Tylenol recalls in the last few years that have undermined confidence in the brand. Recalls will make headlines, and social media only makes it faster for moms to hear about it. While product recalls are difficult for a brand, transparency is crucial to rebuilding trust with Millennial consumers.

In 2006, when Mattel was faced with a lead paint issue in toys, they created voluntary safety recalls in what was the largest toy recall in the history of manufacturing. They stayed in front of the issue by setting up a voluntary safety recall information website that was updated regularly. Messages from the chairman and CEO appeared on the website and product-specific information was readily available. The company communicated often, sincerely and transparently — tactics that did not go unnoticed by Millennials.

Historical events of her childhood once again play a role in how the Millennial Mom behaves as a consumer. Events such as the Columbine shootings and 9/11 have instilled a fear of the unknown in these women. She wants to know what can be expected from brands and she wants the clear facts on what she is getting in your product.

Millennial Moms are label readers for this reason: enter transparency. They want to know exactly what is in your product and how it will affect their families.

## #TakeNote

Moms are watching and if they see you claim to be supportive of families and your company policy says otherwise, they will never trust you or your brand again. It's important to ensure that all aspects of your brand are aligned before communicating with Millennial Moms.

Another must for marketers who want to connect with Millennial Moms is to know what you expect from them. For instance, if you decide to introduce moms to your brand by inviting Mom Bloggers to your national headquarters, make sure you have a plan in place for what happens after the moms leave your office. They will ask what you want in return, I assure you of that! If you run a social media promotion or campaign that requires an action like posting a photo or tweeting with a hashtag, make sure you're clear on the requirements and outcome of their actions. The Millennial Mom is open to a meaningful relationship with your brand but she wants that engagement to be built on mutual respect and transparency. One of the best ways to establish transparency is to allow experienced brand executives to manage social media channels. All too often this important communication is given to interns. Moms can see right through this.

## #21 R-E-S-P-E-C-T.

Aretha Franklin spelled it out well before its time. Respect is exactly what Millennial Moms expect from the people with whom they interact. They grew up in the limelight with parents who told them that they could achieve their greatest dreams. As adults, they expect to be given the respect that is earned when someone is destined for greatness. They have opinions and expect you to not only listen, but also to respect the knowledge and thoughtfulness behind it. I'm going to show how they express opinions in several of the Facts discussed later in this book, but for now I'll summarize it with the Fact that they want you to respect them.

### #TakeNote

Brands have a unique opportunity to leverage this quality of Millennial Moms since sharing helps generate buzz in the Mom Market. Engage with your best Millennial Mom customers and empower them to share their opinions about your product with you. Give them a platform to express their thoughts with other prospective customers. For example, HP was looking for a way to engage Millennial Moms in the crafting space as content providers on their website myprintly.com. They came to BSM Media for help. Well-established crafting moms were handpicked as highlighted experts to receive exclusive information and access to the HP team. The program projected that these women would provide relevant content for the site and social media sharing to the tune of 500,000 online impressions. After the first quarter in existence, not only had they provided over 40 pieces of content, but the 14 moms had also generated over 1.2 million online impressions for the brand. The Millennial Moms repaid the respect HP showed them with intense social sharing. Sometimes it's better to develop deep relationships built on mutual respect with a few key Millennial influencers rather than casting a net to a large, uninvolved ist of Millennial mothers.

## #22 Respect goes both ways.

It starts with a respect for her own parents and then spreads out to her grandparents and even further to her friends. She recognizes that the society she lives in now was largely shaped by the efforts of others. She remembers how her mother climbed the corporate ladder and shattered the glass ceiling for other generations and she's heard the stories of her grandfather who fought in WWII. Best of all, the Millennial recognizes that these people provided her with the education and confidence to do great things with her own life. She expresses her gratitude through respect. Millennials also believe that it's their duty to provide elder care for their parents. Even as young adults, they have an expectation that they will do this and plan for the emotional and financial responsibilities.

The respect that Millennial Moms have for their elders transcends to the brands that these people used and loved as well. This is great news for older or nostalgic brands. What's old is new and in demand among Millennials. You don't have to go further than Christmas 2014 to see examples of this. Polaroid cameras were sold out on Amazon. Vera Bradley backpacks were the hot item for college-aged girls and anything from Lilly Pulitzer was on the list of sorority Millennials. The frenzy that Target created in spring 2015 by offering Lilly Pulitzer in their stores is one example of the love Millennials have for recognizing older brands. Hasbro has updated Mr. Potato Head to attract the attention of young adults. Millennial families supplement Battleship, Twister and Candy Land apps with family game night by using physical editions of these popular games. Even old music is making a comeback with Millennials who played Bon Jovi and Boston on Guitar Hero.

## #TakeNote

There are ways for brands to leverage a Millennial Mom's admiration for the people and things that came before her. Bringing your company's history to the forefront of your marketing efforts can be an effective strategy in the Mom Market in several ways. First, she likes knowing you have a rich heritage with customers. Second, she wants transparency. Your history illustrates what you stand for, and how you got your start is part of the transparency of your relationship. It's easy to turn these strategies into tactics.

If you are a brand with a history, Throwback Thursday (#TBT) is a great way to connect with the Millennial Mom on Twitter or Facebook. Just last week, I noticed a photo on my Facebook page with Delta flight attendants in old uniforms and the #TBT hashtag. A simple photo that effectively communicated that Delta had a long history of serving its customers had been shared over 200 times and received 50 comments. Peg Perego posts photos of old strollers online as an effective way to communicate their 50-year history. Ask moms to post photos of themselves using your product as a child or of family traditions that included your product. Such tactics allow her to reminisce with her family and remember how your brand was a part of her childhood.

# #23 Change is a constant in the lives of Millennial Moms.

They change their wireless devices almost as often as they change their clothes. In fact, Apple made it cool to change. Millennial Moms are very comfortable with change. It has been happening around them since they were born in the 80s and 90s. Let's look at a Millennial Mom who was born in 1980. She called friends on a landline phone until her parents gave her a cell phone for emergencies. After the launch of the Internet, text messages emerged during her teen years. Today, she carries more than one wireless device in her diaper bag and likely has one for her child as well. She likes change. She expects it. This is good news and bad news for brands.

Compared to previous generations, #MillennialMoms are more open to and accepting of change when it comes to their favorite brands.

The good news is that Millennial Moms will tolerate and even accept rebranding, repackaging and new product launches. Soup doesn't have to come in a can and baby food doesn't have to come in a jar. In fact, these changes, such as serving food in pouches, are viewed as progress for Millennial Moms. For innovative brands who churn out new products often, the Millennial Moms are the perfect consumer for you.

The bad news is that Millennial Moms expect and desire your brand to change often. Thanks to the expectations of Millennials who want "new" flavors and changes from the old brands they love, we now have birthday cake-, mint-, and peanut butter-flavored Oreos. Consumers can now find tomato basil- and chicken tortilla-flavored Campbell's soups on the store shelves in bags rather than cans. For brands whose corporate culture won't allow them to change rapidly, the Millennial Mom can be a challenge. It's important to find the right balance of offering the Millennial Mom her favorite go-to designs and flavors but also presenting enough variety to keep her excited about your brand.

# #24 Relationships are really important to the Millennial Mom.

There is probably no other word that holds as much importance in effective marketing to mothers than the word "relationship." It's a word that appears no fewer than 600 times in my previous books, *Marketing to Moms, Trillion-Dollar Moms* and *Mom 3.0*. It's a word that I typically tie to adjectives such as "relevant," "timely," "meaningful" and "transparent." But for marketers like myself, the Millennial Moms have upped the ante. They take the demand for a relationship to a whole new level.

The Millennial Mom has enjoyed meaningful relationships since she was a child. Her admiring parents treated her well and made her feel confident in herself. Coaches and educators expressed faith in her talents and offered her support in reaching her goals. The media put her generation in headlines along with words like "the next great generation" and companies raced to befriend her on Facebook. She has relationships with Instagram followers who "like" her outfits, Pinterest followers who repin her favorite foods and text groups who use emojis to express their feelings of joy to her. She has relationships just about everywhere she looks.

There is a challenge for brands to not only establish a relationship with the Millennial Mom, but also create the type of relationship that is engaging, transparent and relevant to her. It seems like it should be easy with all the tools we have at our disposal. Facebook allows us to see what she posts, Twitter gives us the chance to follow her conversations about our products and Pinterest and Instagram illustrate in nearly real time how she is using them. But herein lies the problem: there are thousands of brands using those same tools to get the Millennial Mom's attention. Some say that community chat apps like Snapchat will be the answer, allowing us to have one-on-one relationships with customers. I suggest examining the tactics you're using and the content you're delivering to her.

Marketers who are still spending thousands on gaining "likes" on their Facebook page are wasting money. "Likes" on Facebook remind me of the data hubs once possessed by car manufacturers. Companies like Ford and Chrysler have terabytes of data on individual customers, yet only use about 5% of it to maintain their current customers. Ask any of my clients my views on data collection. If you don't know what you're going to do with the information, there's no need to collect it from the consumer. It's that simple. If you can't define how you will use the "like" or what it means to your overall marketing plan, then it's worthless. What does a "like" really mean for a brand and why do Millennial Moms "like" certain pages? We asked a few for you:

*"I am actually pretty picky about who I like. I don't want to get slammed with a lot of ads in my feed so I have to truly love the brand and feel like they are essential. I won't like a page just for a coupon, free sample or similar. It has to be a brand I value and trust. I want to know what is new and upcoming as well as see behind the scenes."*—Coralie S., 30

*"I want to see their products outside of their website. Some brands feature customer photos and reviews (on Facebook), which I appreciate when making a decision to purchase."*—Katie D., 34

*"I follow brands that are relevant and important to my stage in life. I stick around when they are engaging and provide great content, not always just about their product. Coupons are great too but the content is essential to maintain my interest."*—Wendy W., 32

*"I think it's essential that brands allow posts to their FB wall. I realize it may not all be positive, but I have much more respect for a brand that allows for easy feedback. At a social media conference recently a keynote speaker talked about that (responses/conversation, crisis management, etc., and how that builds trust much more than just even the best product/service). Not even three weeks later I experienced it as a consumer and the advice was spot-on."*—Jennifer K., 33

*"I like following brands when they are engaging. Maybe not with me as an individual, but with their followers in general. It's nice when their posts are informative, humorous, and creative. If a brand is boring or just advertising, I won't hesitate to unlike."*—Virginia M., 29

*"When I 'like' a brand, that's an invitation for them to share things with me that I would want including coupon codes, recipe*

*ideas, entertaining videos, etc. When brands pollute my stock photos of their product or random photos of peop. fun in the office at corporate headquarters, I unlike them that invitation."—Carly M., 35*

"*I like a brand when they post interesting articles or c ways to use their product — i.e., my kids' music lesson group posts stuff about the effect of music on kids and long- term benefits of music lessons."—Sierra R., 32*

## #TakeNote

Relationships between a brand and a Millennial Mom are so important that I suggest you don't start one until you have a very clear plan on how you intend to maintain it. You only have one shot when it comes to the Millennial, so it'd better be transparent and it'd better be real. There are several effective tactics a marketer can use to establish and maintain a meaningful relationship with Millennial Moms. One of my favorites is establishing Mom Ambassador programs and using them as content providers; I'll discuss more tactics in greater detail later in this book.

## #25 Greatness is her destiny.

The idea of a purposeful life is a key motivator for the Millennial Mom. The desire to do great things can be seen in blogs focused on social good, Facebook pages committed to helping other mothers, products invented by Millennial Moms and online petitions seeking political change, to name just a few. According to a Pew Research study, 96% of Millennials said they intend to do something great.

An outcome of her pursuit of greatness might be the YOLO (You Only Live Once) attitude. She knows she only has one life and it can be cut short, so she has to live it to the fullest. Terms such as "Just Do It" worked for Nike in connecting with the Gen Xers. However, Millennials want to do it but do it better than anyone else. One of the most popular terms used by Millennials is "Be a Rockstar" because "Just Do It" isn't enough.

## Millennial Moms Doing Great Things

**Jessica Alba**
Mom of 2
Co-Founder, The Honest Company

The Honest Company produces a nontoxic line of baby and household products. Launched in 2012, the company is now valued at nearly $1 billion.

**Alicia Keys**
Mom of 2
Co-Founder, Keep A Child Alive Foundation

The Keep A Child Alive Foundation raises funds to provide care, food, and support services for children and families in Africa and India affected by AIDS.

**Desiree Vargas Wrigley**
Mom of 2, Stepmom of 1
Co-Creator, GiveForward.com

GiveForward.com allows individuals to raise money to rebuild after a natural disaster, cover medical expenses, or even grant the wishes of sick children. The website has raised over $160 million since its inception.

**Lisa Hallet**
Mom of 3
Co-Founder, Wear Blue: Run to Remember

Wear Blue: Run to Remember is a national nonprofit that aims to honor the American military through running. Created in 2010, after Lisa's husband was killed in action in Afghanistan in August 2009.

## #26 Millennial Moms are pragmatic.

They base their decisions on facts and logical thinking rather than theory. This might come from the amount of research they do. They gather facts and make a decision. So does this mean that brands need to apply pragmatic marketing to connect with the pragmatic consumer? Quite the contrary. Setting standard marketing practices will not work with this generation of mothers. Applying a rigid marketing process with little room for change and customization will be met with hesitation by Millennial Moms. They want your marketing efforts to be practical but also to enhance their relationships with you at the same time.

## #27 Education is valued by Millennial Moms.

While her parents were pushing her to the stars, they pushed her to college. Her parents' expectations, struggles finding a job and the demands of a knowledge-based economy have all contributed to a record enrollment in graduate schools. High-school graduation rates among Millennials is at a two-decade high of 72%, with 68% of those armed with a high-school diploma heading for college.[8]

From the start, parents of Millennials told them that they were capable of anything and graduating from college was a must. In fact, helicopter mothers likely helped Millennial daughters fill out applications for higher education. The Millennial Mom values education as a means for reaching her full potential and she has a deep desire to keep learning.

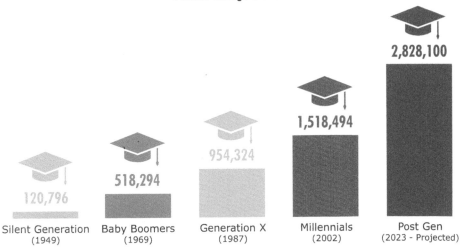

**Female College Graduates**

| Silent Generation (1949) | Baby Boomers (1969) | Generation X (1987) | Millennials (2002) | Post Gen (2023 - Projected) |
|---|---|---|---|---|
| 120,796 | 518,294 | 954,324 | 1,518,494 | 2,828,100 |

## #28 She is teachable.

Because she values education, it means she is teachable. She's open to new things and approaches learning with confidence. In fact, education is one of the most important political issues according to our research on Millennial Moms. The value she puts on education is passed down to her children. She seeks out ways to give her child a head start on reading, math and science. Her love of learning can also be seen in the Do-It-Yourself space and most visibly in her posts on Pinterest.

## #TakeNote

Brands can use technology to introduce new ways to use a product. Pinterest is great for this, as well as Vine. I recently watched Kathy Cano-Murillo from www.CraftyChica.com demonstrate how to make a Valentine's Day craft on Vine. I have to admit when she first told me that she would use Vine

10-second how-to video, I was skeptical. Then I
r do it and was amazed at the results. In just 30
thy's Vine video had more than 10,000 views.
's an incredible return on investment in terms of
banner impressions. Millennial Moms like to learn and
they are willing to search out new ways of completing old
tasks on YouTube, Vine, Pinterest, Facebook and Instagram.

## #29 Millennials appear to be living smaller than their parents but are mindful of material things.

In fact, even frugal Millennials are purchasing high-end brands like Michael Kors, Tory Burch and Hunter. They are a financially cautious generation who are putting off the purchase of their first home and a new car but will splurge on a designer handbag or new iPhone.

 #MillennialMoms live smaller than their parents.

Once they decide to leave home, they are moving to urban areas with affordable lofts and townhouses where shopping and entertainment are accessible by foot rather than by car. Since 1920, growth within U.S. cities outpaces the growth outside U.S. cities. This trend is spawning the concept of "urban burbs" or the redevelopment of urban environments with walkable down-towns.[9] In welcome news to realtors, when Millennials decide to buy a home, they are skipping over a starter house and going straight to the family home.

## #30 Traditional shock value has been desensitized but not eliminated.

In an attempt to reach influential Millennials, many brands go outside of the box with edgy, push-the-envelope video and social media campaigns. It works most of the time for Millen-nials, who are often seen as a desensitized audience and sport a "whatever works" attitude. (Do we have violent video games to thank for this?) However, sometimes outside of the box goes too far. Just ask Nationwide Insurance and GoDaddy.

In what has been dubbed the "Super Bowl Bummer" of 2015, Nationwide Insurance aired a video aimed at raising awareness for preventable childhood accidents. The backlash was fierce. The video, featuring a young boy talking about the firsts he will never experience because he died, went too far even for Millennials. With a goal of starting a conversation about preventable childhood accidents, Nationwide defended the (very expensive) spot. It certainly started a conversation, just not the one that was intended.[10]

GoDaddy also aired a sneak peek of a Super Bowl ad, titled "Journey Home," that was met with harsh criticism for being insensitive about animal welfare, and specifically the plight of dogs from puppy mills and disreputable breeders. In what many experts say was an unprecedented move, GoDaddy pulled the ad from the 2015 Super Bowl lineup with a subsequent and hasty apology by CEO Blake Irving.[11] Go Daddy has social media to thank for the wake-up call regarding the sensitivities of Millennials.

## #31 They are politically active.

Politics is a subject that is often ignored in discussions about the power of moms. It gained some attention when Soccer Moms were credited with helping Bill Clinton get elected in 1992. Every presidential election season, I conduct research in hopes of shining a light on the power of mom voters. Time and time again moms tell us that they have an interest in politics that also influences the views of family and friends. Boomer moms told us as far back as 2001 that they spoke to an average of seven moms a week about a political topic. Generation X moms focused their political interests on global issues such as world peace and saving the environment. Millennial Moms are focused on issues that are a little closer to home.

According to our research, education and healthcare rank the highest in importance of political issues, followed close behind by poverty and human rights. It's no wonder that Hillary Clinton has Millennials as her top priority for votes in the 2016 presidential campaign. Prior to the last election, 85% of Millennial Moms who responded to a BSM Media survey had planned to vote. When Millennials vote, they tend to vote Democratic and support a more liberal view on issues like gay marriage and the legalization of marijuana.

**The Top Two Most Important Political Issues of Millennial Moms**

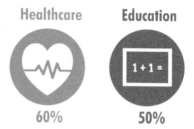

**Healthcare** — 60%

**Education** — 50%

## #32 Millennials are socialists or at least act like it.

Occupy Wall Street, anticorporate movements and a push for government programs all have the fingerprints of Millennials on them. A poll by the marketing firm Good shows that 49% of Millennials view socialism in a favorable way compared to 43% who view it unfavorably. However, they may not label themselves as socialists. In a 2014 Pew Research report, 50% of Millennials described themselves as Independents. It seems almost logical that the children of Baby Boomers would think in this manner. They grew up in a prosperous time and reaped the material benefits of a good economy. On the other hand, the older Millennials suffered through a recession that hit them hard. They know what happens when greed makes a mark on the economy. They watched their parents lose their homes, jobs and retirement funds. It's not a pretty picture and it disappoints them.

## #33 Religion is on the decline among Millennials.

This fact may surprise many readers. In fact, it surprised me. When I studied the upcoming Millennial Moms while writing *Trillion-Dollar Moms: Marketing to a New Generation of Mothers (Kaplan Business, March 2005)*, I predicted a very religious generation of mothers. I made this prediction based on the rising popularity of gospel rock music among teenage

Millennials. I also presumed that a generation so €
volunteerism and philanthropy would gravitate to
religion. My assumptions were wrong and the research
it. A Pew Research Social & Demographic Trends rep‹
that almost 30% are not affiliated with any religion,
than older adults when they were the same ages.

In the same report, Pew Research noted that this decline is
the highest disaffiliation of any generation since they began
asking the question a quarter century ago. It seems that the Millennials' acceptance of diversity plays a role in this decline. They
have been turned off from church positions on topics like gay
marriage. To a Millennial who is accepting of all people and the
values they bring along with them, this issue has been confusing
and in some cases polarizing.

If you are particularly interested in the topic of Millennials
and religion, I highly recommend *The Millennials: Connecting
to America's Largest Generation" (B&H Books, 2011)* by Thom
S. Rainer and Jess W. Rainer. The authors are self-proclaimed
born-again Christians and tie a great deal of their research to
religious implications.

## #34 The Millennial Mom is collaborative and inclusive.

She likes to be connected and enjoys relationships. Her peers
are a diverse group of individuals who bring a variety of values
with them. Collaborating is just another way of deepening the
relationships that are important to her and perhaps a means to
discovering new ones.

### #TakeNote

This is great news for brands! Millennial Moms are not
only open to collaborating with companies on spreading news,
deals and product information but they actually invite it.
When you are strategizing marketing tactics, consider ones
that invite moms to join you in supporting causes, creating
new designs or deciding on the next product innovation.
Chick-fil-A has found success with and growth of their kids'
meals by using their Mom Ambassadors to help decide on the
toys included in future meals.

## 35 Images are important to Millennial Moms.

One of the elements I work hard to deliver to clients is my access to experts. This is one of those times I want share my access to a professional whom I respect and who has unique insights about the world of Millennial Moms and images. Meet Millennial Noah Lomax. He's an expert on his cohort and currently works as a manager in the photo imaging and printing industry at HP. I posed the question to him: "Why are images so important to Millennial Moms?"

"It's no secret — Millennials love pictures," Noah answered. "Almost 90% snap at least one picture a week on their mobile device. 1.8 million of these photos are uploaded to social media daily. While the act of taking pictures and sharing them is not new, it has clearly grown into a phenomenon. Today's photos are liked, shared, commented on, turned into memes, and even used to start national and global movements."

Noah went on: "To understand why Millennials take so many pictures, we have to start at the core. Millennials place an extremely high value on relationships and connectivity. Sharing, engaging with and 'liking' photos gives them a very tangible outlet for this value. Photos allow them to quickly capture, reflect and share their favorite moments in ways that words cannot express. The #TBT, Throwback Thursday, is one of most well-known displays of this desire. What they share is determined by asking three questions:

• 'Who was involved?' They are more likely to share if something was done with friends.

• 'How remarkable was their experience?' If they traveled somewhere exotic, met someone famous, ate something delicious or had the extreme negative alternative to any of these situations, they are very likely to share that information.

• 'What is their current mood?' If they are feeling celebratory, extroverted, expressive, needing validation, lonely, indecisive, nostalgic or even intoxicated, there is a higher likelihood they are going to post.

"Where they share," Noah continued, "is determined by the appropriateness of the photo and the possible audience of the platform. Less-appropriate photos that they don't want the entire world to see might be reserved for texting or Snapchat, while nostalgic memories they want to commemorate will likely land on Facebook, Instagram or even printed in 'Polaroid' form.

"This core value of connectedness is only the first piece. The industry growth is driven psychologically but enabled technologically. When asked, 'What do you love about taking pictures?' the most common reasons Millennials gave were convenience and improved image quality.

"'I always have my phone with me.' The camera on my phone is 'small and portable, has good picture quality [and I] can do some photo editing if needed.'

"As social media platforms grew, smartphone makers differentiated themselves by improving their cameras as well as integrating Facebook and Twitter into their native apps. This reinforced an end-user behavior of grabbing and sharing more than ever before. In an almost cyclical effect, new platforms like Instagram and Snapchat entered the scene and new viral behaviors appeared like selfies, mini-videos, ugly selfies and even 'belfies' (the infamous butt selfie). Then came Vine and Periscope and continued improvements to phone cameras. The end is nowhere in sight. So what is the key takeaway for marketers?

When you match quality and convenience with the #MillennialMom's core value of connectedness you will tap into big business and new markets.

"Slowly and somewhat reluctantly, companies are starting to accept the new, diverse behaviors of this generation — selfies included. Some businesses have made the costly mistake of mocking the generation's behavior. I would advise against this. The Millennial generation has $200 billion in direct purchase power and $500 billion in indirect purchase power ... annually. Observe what they do and then seek to understand why they do it and you will undoubtedly see the ROI in your business. When in doubt, ask them. If there's one thing a Millennial likes more than taking and sharing photos, it's being asked for their opinion."

Perhaps this is why Noah was more than willing to share his thoughts on images with me for this book.

## #36 Millennials are creative and not afraid to try DIY.

Millennial Moms are innovative, creative and they aren't afraid to take on a new project. Thanks to Pinterest, YouTube and empowerment TV shows like Rachael Ray's and *The Chew*, they can fix a gourmet meal after they assemble IKEA furniture and paint the nursery. Yes, Millennial Moms are fearless. And they aren't afraid to laugh at their failures with a hashtag like #PinterestFail.

They reuse, redefine and recycle products to find new uses for them. Shows like Lara Spencer's *Flea Market Flip* and DIY shows like *Extreme Makeover* inspire creativity and confidence. The Millennial Mom takes friendly competition to a whole new level as she searches Pinterest for birthday party ideas and wedding presents or sells homemade crafts on Etsy. What she is doing well, another Millennial Mom will enhance and do better and share it with her followers. Nothing is off limits when it comes to things she can piece together into something new. Long after she's done with your product she may be using your packaging in ways you never imagined. The best way to discover what the multipurpose mom is doing with your product is to search Pinterest. You may be very surprised at what you find. In fact, you may discover new ways to promote and sell your product by watching how moms are using it in crafty applications.

### Daytime Television Shows That Empower Millennial Moms

| Live with Kelly and Michael | The Ellen DeGeneres Show |
| Rachael Ray Show | The Talk |
| Steve Harvey | The View |
| The Chew | The Wendy Williams Show |

# #TakeNote

There are several important marketing impl[ ]
this Millennial behavior. First, brands should hav[ ]
assembly and setup videos for each and every pr[ ]
sell. These can be a combination of consumer-generated videos
and brand-created content. Along the same lines, I recommend
videos on how to use your product. Keep them short and sweet,
but informative. She might not read the instructions but she'll
watch your video. Next, encourage her use of your product in
ways you never intended, as long as it's safe, ethical and moral,
of course. Send product to crafters and invite them to let their
creativity go wild. I did this recently for a cooler painting company called The Cooler Nation. The company produces
decoration-ready coolers that can be used as gifts. It's a cool
concept and I invite you to check it out at www.thecoolerna-
tion.com. We sent coolers to craft bloggers and DIY Viners.
They were so excited about the opportunity to show off their
talents that they posted their finished products to an audience
of 1.2 million over their social media outlets.

Finally, if you find a mom on Pinterest who uses your
product frequently, reach out to her and see how you might
strengthen the relationship. If she's already a fan, she may be
open to creating digital content for distribution on your social
media pages. Apply some of the same creativity that Millennial
Moms are exhibiting to your marketing plans and you may
find a pearl of an idea you never saw before.

*Millennial Moms grew up overscheduled, so now they use technology to control the many demands on their time.*

# CHAPTER
## 2

# Millennials as Moms

**#37** **Only 1/3 of all Millennial women are currently moms, according to U.S. Census numbers.**

The cohort of Millennial Moms just keeps growing. The delay of motherhood common among Millennial women, combined with the fact that the young end of this generation is just reaching their 20s, means that the impact of this generation of moms has not yet been fully felt. Without doubt the landscape and conversations will evolve as the majority of these tech-savvy women become mothers.

**#38** **Millennials are postponing motherhood.**

The average Millennial is 26 when she gives birth,[1] the oldest average age yet for first-time motherhood and two years older than the average age in the mid-90s. In Europe, the age of new moms has risen to 33 years old and a BabyCenter report shows 28.5 as the age of first-time motherhood among Canadian women.[2]

**#39** **Millennials perceive themselves in a positive light.**

---

**How Millennial Moms Perceive Themselves**

Tech Savvy    Fearless    Family Oriented    Entrepreneurial    Social
Entitled    Creative    Spoiled    Forward-Thinking
Open-Minded    Selfish    Influential    Ambitious    Innovative
Modern    Hopeful    Trendy    Resourceful    Tolerant
Connected    Energetic    Empowered    Caring    Loyal

---

## #40 Millennial Moms can be critical of Gen Xers.

> How Millennial Moms Perceive Generation X Moms
>
> Wise **Old-Fashioned** Pessimistic Naive
> Hardworking Cynical Mature **Uptight** Smart
> Outspoken **Family-Oriented** Closed-Minded
> **Responsible** Dependable **Stubborn**

## #41 Millennial Moms view Baby Boomers with a sense of respect.

> How Millennial Moms Perceive Baby Boomers
>
> **Family-Oriented** Modest
> Carefree Naive **Fortunate** Smart
> Independent **Frugal** Traditional **Domestic**
> **Old-Fashioned** Peaceful **Laid-Back**
> Hardworking **Stubborn**

## #42 Boomers and Gen Xers perceive Millennial Moms as entitled.

> How Other Generations of Moms Perceive Millennials
>
> Entitled **Creative** Tech Savvy
> Immature **Wise** Tolerant **Lazy** **Relaxed**
> **Adaptable** Dependant Proactive **Naive**
> Confident **Egotistical** Misguided Carefree
> **Spoiled** Sensitive

# #43 Millennials don't agree with the negative stereotypes of their generation.

As I mention in Fact #39, Millennial Moms see themselves in a very positive light. Sure, they have a few flaws. What generation doesn't? These moms feel that they are unjustly being labeled with terms like "entitled," "lazy" and "selfish." This is very different from the creative, resourceful and inspiring woman they see in the mirror.

*"Millennials are often characterized as lazy. When I look at my Millennial peers, I see people who are giving multitasking a whole new meaning — particularly when it comes to juggling career responsibilities and parenting responsibilities. There's nothing lazy about seeking work-life balance."—Maria M., 35*

# #44 The role of mother takes on a new definition.

While the world was telling the Millennial female about the value of children, the Gen X moms and a few early-adoption Baby Boomers were communicating the "coolness" of motherhood. In 2000, the oldest Millennial women were about 20 years old and looking forward to the future with a desire to have children in their lives. Enter the Mommy Blogger. By the way, I am not a fan of the title "Mommy Blogger" and my dislike of the term is supported by ample research that says Mommy Bloggers don't like it either. However, this is the term most used in 2000, so that's why you're seeing it here.

Generation X moms who predominantly were at home with children began chronicling their lives as a mother. The motivation for most of these women was not to create a cultural shift in the value marketers place on moms, but we all know what happened. They intended to use newly introduced technology to keep distant relatives and friends updated on the lives of their children. A blog was a way to easily share photos, milestones and special occasions. Along the way they discovered that blogs could also provide much- needed adult friendship and input on products and parenting dilemmas. Mom Bloggers soon branded themselves with creative names like ScaryMommy, Girl'sGoneChild and SelfishMom. Motherhood became cool, and, more important for the pragmatic Millennial, it seemed manageable thanks to the pages and pages of information she could find on Mommy Blogs. No longer did motherhood appear to be a one-size-fits-all phase of life. It was a customizable experience that allowed her to develop a relationship with a child in her own way. Becoming a mother brought together a lot of the attitudes that came naturally to a Millennial woman: a fondness for her own mother, the value of having a child, the hope a child represents for the future and the desire for greatness which could be accomplished by leaving her mark on the world through a child.

#45 **Millennial Moms see themselves as more prepared for parenting because of their access to information.**

64% of the Millennial Moms in our survey say they see themselves as prepared or more prepared for motherhood compared to their mother's generation. Much of the credit is given to the accessibility to technology.

*"I've been more prepared for parenting than my parents were, but in some respects that was not a good thing. Most of the answers to your parenting concerns are a click away, but that can lead to becoming overwhelmed and decision paralysis. I think parents nowadays are less likely to parent from their instincts. Instead, we parent by committee, leaning on our friends' experiences, blogs, social media, etc."—Tara J., 32*

*"Millennial Moms have been overwhelmed with information since birth since we're the first generation who have had access to computers since childhood. (I got my first Apple computer in 1988 when I turned 5!) The great advantage this gives us as parents is that over the course of our lives we've processed an unbelievable amount of parenting-related media sound bites, personal recollections, research reports, and expert guides. Instead of having one book on how to get my child to sleep, I have 30 blog entries from moms in the trenches, 10 e-books from the hottest sleep experts, 15 YouTube videos demonstrating bedtime rituals, and 4 podcasts to fall back on if none of that works (not to mention the child development classes I took in college that I'm still paying for). On the*

*one hand, it might seem like we're overcomplicating the simple task of motherhood, but I feel like I've been gifted with so many more tools than my mom had."—Carly M., 35*

*"As a child, I grew up with two sets of encyclopedias on the bookshelf, which were quickly replaced by a family desktop computer and the Internet as I became a teenager. With the boom of technology that came along with the close of the 20th century, more information and knowledge was at our fingertips than ever before, and I loved it. It made me feel prepared for anything, because I could research a situation until I was blue in the face, trying to understand every outcome and possibility. Naturally, when I became pregnant with my son, my research and reading continued, not only about my pregnancy and birth, but also parenting during the early years. Although every baby is different and each family has its own unique solution to each situation, I take the challenges of parenting one step at a time, combining my instinct, lots of reading and my mother's own recommendations. My mom has often told me what a 'quarter-life crisis' panic she had, realizing she was going to have another human besides herself to care for, but I don't remember having that anxiety before my children were born. I'm not sure if I feel 'more' prepared than my own mother, but I most certainly feel more comfortable about it, and I certainly credit that to the age in which I was born. Technology can certainly cause us to waste time, become paranoid about conditions or cause our attention to be sucked into a machine, but used for 'good,' I find that humanity's collective brain and experience can offer a lot for the nervous, unprepared, or curious parent, like myself."—Lindsey P., 34*

## #46 Millennial Moms want smaller families.

It may be the effect of the economy. It might be their pragmatic nature. It may be that they are waiting longer to have their first child or deciding to have children out of wedlock. There could be a number of reasons that Millennial women consider fewer children as the perfect-size family. According to our research, 32% of Millennial Moms said that two children is the right-size family. Over 39% of our Gen X moms responded that three or more was the perfect number of children, compared to only 30% of Millennials.

**Average Number of Children Per Household**

#47 **Being a good parent is more important than being a good spouse.**

A 2011 Pew Research survey found that 52% of Millennials said being a good parent is "one of the most important things" in life. Just 30% say the same about having a successful marriage. That's compared to 42% and 35%, respectively, of the previous generation (Gen X) who said in 1997, when they were about the same age as Millennials in 2010, that being a good parent and having a successful marriage were the most important things in life.[3]

#48 **She co-parents more than any other generation.**

It took a village of nannies, daycare providers and grandparents for her mother to raise her, but for Millennial Moms who decide to marry, the support in parenting comes from her spouse. Thankfully, the Millennial Dad has a desire to demonstrate his confidence in his ability to take on parenting tasks. Among the daily tasks of parenting, the chores most often shared by both parents are diapering, homework, drop-off/pick-up and bedtime routines. Millennial Moms seem to assume more responsibility in the areas of grocery shopping, staying home with sick kids, and morning routines, although cooking is a chore that is widely shared between Millennial Moms and Millennial Dads. According to our research, almost 26% of Millennial Moms feel they split the duties of a parent equally between them and their partners.

More fathers are now doing the household grocery shopping, which leaves the older moms asking, "Where were these men when we had babies?" In fact, more than half — 57% — of our Millennial Moms believe the workload of their parents was divided unequally, with their mothers taking on more than 60% of day-to-day tasks.

Yes, Millennial Moms get help from Millennial Dads but the best part is that they are willing to accept it as well. Her Baby Boomer mother with her martyr-like, guilt-ridden approach to life probably would have turned down the help had her spouse offered to take the kids for the night.

## #TakeNote

Millennial Moms who enjoy collaboration make a great mate for co-parenting. So what does this mean for marketers? It means that she relates to commercials and ads that showcase the involved dad. It means that marketers should consider that, unlike Gen Xers and Baby Boomers, the Millennial Mom is likely to be sending her spouse to the store to pick up more than the milk. Now does this mean you as a marketer should run out and refocus all of your marketing strategies to include dads? The answer is no. Moms still make the majority of household buying decisions.

An even more likely scenario is that the Millennial parents are shopping together. Tide recently ran a commercial during an episode of *Shark Tank* that featured a Millennial Dad doing the laundry with his preschool daughter who had spilled juice on her favorite princess costume. It was "spot on" (pun intended) because not only did it appeal to dads but gained the applause of Millennial Moms who are likely to be the purchaser of Tide.

# #49 She wants to replicate her own childhood with her children.

**Areas Moms Would Like to Replicate From Their Childhood When Raising Their Own Children**

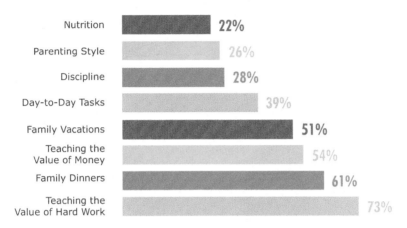

| | |
|---|---|
| Nutrition | 22% |
| Parenting Style | 26% |
| Discipline | 28% |
| Day-to-Day Tasks | 39% |
| Family Vacations | 51% |
| Teaching the Value of Money | 54% |
| Family Dinners | 61% |
| Teaching the Value of Hard Work | 73% |

# #50 Move over, household CEO, the COO is here.

Gen Xers preferred to call themselves the household CEO, but Millennials see themselves more in a logistical role as the chief operating officer. We've been asking moms about the titles that describe her role in the family for almost two decades. For the first time ever, moms proposed the term "cofounder." In fact, the title was the second most popular choice among Millennial Moms. My guess is that it's a sign of the importance she puts on the family unit and the increased involvement of the Millennial Dad.

# #51 Her role models are her own parents.

This is very different from the Gen Xer who separated herself from her parents. Research shows that the Millennial Mom likes the involvement of her mother and will turn to her for advice on everything from finances to relationships. Her parents no longer have to be helicopter parents because they have trained their Millennial children to return on their own. In many ways the Millennial Mom wants to be the newer, more educated, more technologically savvy, more socially connected version of

**She's More Than "Mom"**

her own mother. She wants to do it her way but admires how her own mother did it years ago. Boomers proudly tout deep friendships with their Millennial daughters and vice versa.

Almost 42% of Millennial Moms say they chat with their own mothers daily, compared to 32% of Gen Xers who do the same. More than 84% of Millennial Mothers responded that they talk to her at least 2 – 3 times a week.

Millennial Moms are consulting their mothers with parenting questions at a rate of 36%. In fact, unlike the Gen Xer who sought advice from the pediatrician, Millennials will call their mother first.

## #52 Millennial Moms also want their parents to be involved in the lives of their children.

Even though the parent/child relationship has changed with Boomers and their children, Millennials like their parents and hope that their own children will find the emotional fulfillment with them that they enjoyed as children. This spells great news for marketers who could potentially see sales from both Millennials and their parents. Millennial Moms are comfortable receiving financial gifts and purchases from their parents. It's estimated that 30% of Boomer grandparents contribute to some household expense of their adult Millennial child. The most popular item for grandparents to subsidize is tuition, followed by extracurricular activities and childcare. Big-ticket items like family travel are also categories where we see grandparents purchasing on behalf of their Millennial children and grandchildren. In the mall she's buying children's clothing and influencing the purchases of her Millennial daughter.

It's likely that travel destinations will continue to see growth in extended family vacations as the Millennial parent seeks out ways to keep her family connected. Marketers with a rich history in the Mom Market should consider focusing some of their marketing budget on the Boomer grandmother as well as the Millennial Mom.

## #53 Grandparents play a different role in the lives of Millennials.

Grandparents play a different role in the lives of Millennial Moms not only for themselves but also for their children. Millennial Moms use their comfort with technology to redefine the relationship between grandparent and grandchild. She uses Skype and FaceTime to deepen the relationship between the two generations that sandwich her. Over 27% of Millennial Moms in our survey said they Skype with their child's grandparents regularly, with another 34% saying the same for FaceTime.

Relationships are important to her and this includes the bond she creates between her children and her own parents. In fact, some Millennial Moms are even willing to purchase technology for grandparents in order to ensure their accessibility to their grandchildren. Last year, in a focus group of Millennial Moms, I asked them about the uses for a wireless printer. More than one mom explained that she had purchased a wireless printer for her mother so that she could email pictures to the printer. One mom explained, "My mom likes to have printed photos of my children but I keep my pictures on my phone, so if I email a photo to her wireless printer, it saves me the work of mailing it." In another focus group, several Millennial Moms explained that they intended to purchase their parents an iPad so that they could Skype with their grandchildren. The desire to stay connected is a two-way street between the Baby Boomer and Millennial. They happily vacation together as has been seen in the rise of what Disney Parks calls "multigenerational travel."

## #TakeNote

For marketers, this means a unique opportunity to sell products and services to two generations of women. The examples I identified were surprising in the technology category, but the opportunity extends to many others such as education, toys and household items. Thirty-four percent of Millennials say that grandparents contribute by purchasing clothing and toys. This is 10% more than the response by Gen X mothers. Almost 8% of grandparents even help with household expenses. When it comes to extracurricular activities and education, grandparents are doing their part as well. On average, 15% of Millennials receive help in these areas. The involvement of Boomer grandparents brings another potential client to the table for you. Boomers and older Gen Xers have more disposable income than their Millennial children and they are more than willing to helicopter over grandkids as much as they did with their children. The Millennial Mom might direct the purchases with the Boomer grandparent footing the bill.

I've already described how important relationships are for the Millennial Moms, and by far the most important relationship is the one she has with her family. Later, when I'm talking about the Millennial Mom and work, I'll discuss how it's the desire to spend time with family that greatly influences the way she works and her desire to earn money.

## #54 Millennial Moms want parental involvement even as adults.

The Millennial Mom welcomes involvement by her parents, but it may be for reasons that surprise you. She's not just looking for parenting advice from her mother. She wants her mother to be available for her own needs in addition to the needs of her child. Remember that a helicopter mother raised today's Millennial Mom. She is accustomed to her mother caring for

her, guiding her through new situations and helpi
plish her goals. She enjoyed being the focus of
attention and is reluctant to give that up as an ad

Now as she enters motherhood, she's not t
mother for recommendations on strollers and baby
she is turning to her mother to explain life insuran
to college accounts and fund family vacations. The good news
for Millennial parents is that their parents are happily available
as many are entering retirement and willing to spend savings
on their children and grandchildren. After all, they've been doing
it their whole life, so why stop now?

## #55  The birth of the shadow parent.

If her mother was a helicopter parent then
Millennial Moms might be called the "shadow
parent." Part of this comes from the availability of
technology to watch her child from the shadows of
social media. Video monitors and apps such as iBaby and
Angelcare monitors allow her to watch her child via a smartphone. The Millennial Mom is following the example of her own
mother's parenting style. After all, she respects her mother so it's
not so bad to follow her parenting style. She is uber-focused on
her children and she wants to stay connected with them.

It comes as no surprise that the moms in our survey told us
that attachment parenting best describes their style of parenting.
A visit to the ABC Baby Expo, the premier show in the baby
product industry, is filled with products that support her desire
to be attached to her child. There are hundreds of baby-wearing
products that facilitate keeping her baby close. I listened to one
young mom tell me while walking the aisle of the show that the
practice of baby-wearing contributes to raising more independent children. I'm not sure whether she is right or wrong but I
found it interesting that the debate even exists.

Safety is one of her motivations in shadowing her children.
They experienced the insecurity of Columbine and the Virginia
Tech massacre as well as 9/11, so they know unexpected things
can happen. As mothers they use video monitors and mobile
viewers, among many other devices. They want their children to

feel safe so they engage with technology that can help them do this from an early age. Millennial Moms might spend a lot of time ensuring the safety of their children and lurking in the shadows, yet they also encourage their children to engage in free play. This type of unstructured play allows the child the freedom to be creative and freethinking about his/her experience with technology and toys. Moms view this as an area that is important to their child's intellectual growth so they tend to step back from controlling the situation. This is an important fact to remember when marketing toys, apps and experiences for her child to the Millennial Moms. She wants to keep her child safe and close but she wants to let her/him explore enough to grow.

*"My parenting style is quite simple: love 'em hard. Early on I would make parenting more difficult than it needed to be. I'd stress about every little decision, worrying late into the night about whether we picked the right school or if they need to be in extracurriculars or if they were getting the right nutrition. But since those early years I've morphed into a more zen version of myself, parenting from a place of love and not fear. If I love my kids with everything I've got, those other decisions become much less important."*—Tara J., 32

*"I am a mother of two with a master's degree in teaching. I have taught preschool, first grade, and university. I place a high value on allowing my children to be who they are, and equipping them to make wise and empowered choices all of their lives. I never force a child to include another one in play, or to give up a prized possession in the name of 'sharing.' We don't do this as adults, and I don't think children should have to do it either! When other children hurt my kids through words or actions, I try to affirm to them that while you can't control the actions of another person, you can control how you let it make you feel. You can control your response to the situation, and you can remove yourself from the source of stress. This is something that I only learned as an adult and I wished that I had learned it when I was six, like my kids. I can't control if my partner, or my boss, or a stranger treats me badly. But I can control my response and I cannot let it ruin my day."*—Candice B., 35

## #56 Millennial Moms create ecosystems of solutions.

Have you ever heard a mom say, "I've got my way of doing

things"? Well, that's her telling you that she has an ecosystem of solutions. Moms bridge together actions, products and behaviors to create easy ways to solve the challenges they have in their daily lives. For example, I know some moms who will grill a chicken on Sunday and use it in three different dinners during the week. Day one will be sliced roasted chicken, followed by a chicken casserole and finally pieces later tossed into a salad. This is an ecosystem for feeding her family.

Another example might be the mom who keeps multiple diaper bags packed for various destinations and occasions such as the playground, beach or church; it's her way of saving time, money and energy. As a brand, it's your job to figure out how you fit into her ecosystems. For instance, if you are a spice or seasoning brand, you might post recipes on Sunday afternoon to give moms suggestions for preparing dinners for the week. If you are a diaper wipe brand, instead of pushing out messages about your absorbency, post how-to videos with easy tips for packing diaper bags for any occasion.

## #TakeNote

The easiest way to identify commonly used ecosystems is to read blogs and browse Pinterest and social media sites. Make a list of all the solutions your product offers moms and search for related content. Using our diaper bag example again, I would search "taking the baby to the beach" or "diaper bags for the beach," combing the results from the latest blog posts and social media mentions for information on how moms are packing your wipes for the beach. On an interesting side note for baby wipe companies, my son, who is in the army, recently told me that I should suggest a valuable opportunity to market the product to soldiers. He explained that soldiers use diaper wipes for bathing when they are in the field. Diaper wipes are part of their ecosystem. The brand manager would likely only learn of this consumer behavior from reading social media posts about their product. This is again why social listening is so important. Listen and read to find opportunities to insert your product into the ecosystem of Millennial Moms.

## #57 Millennial Moms like to have structured lifestyles.

They grew up overscheduled, so now they use technology to control the many demands on their time. Everything is scheduled and they appreciate service providers and brands that make it easy to integrate appointments into their busy lives. In fact, 64% of the Millennial Moms we surveyed said they prefer making appointments without human interaction. Text, email and online scheduling options win big points with moms. Although Millennial Moms are using modern technologies to help manage their schedules, they are also using old-school tools such as wall calendars.

### How Millennial Moms Stay Organized

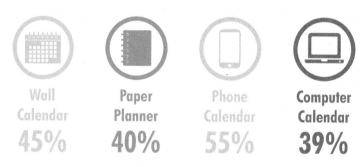

| Wall Calendar | Paper Planner | Phone Calendar | Computer Calendar |
|---|---|---|---|
| 45% | 40% | 55% | 39% |

For a marketer it's more important than ever to get into step with moms. The former generations of moms wanted brands to offer solutions that they could adapt. The Millennial Moms have a schedule and it's important to not only provide the solution, but also insert your solution into that schedule. Let's look at an example for those offering a food solution. We know that Millennial Moms cruise through Pinterest in the early afternoon looking for dinner ideas. As a food provider, I would make sure that you have updated pinned ideas for quick dinner solutions. Insert your brand and solution into the schedule that she keeps for herself and her family. As a bonus, it's a first step in developing a valuable relationship.

# #58 When it comes to juggling life, like mother like daughter.

Millennial Moms watched their Boomer mothers blaze the trail of work-life balance and have mastered their own skills through the use of technology. They are willing to pay for lifestyle management tools and turn to apps to help them through their busiest days. Unlike their own mothers, who relied on friends and family to help manage the demands of work and family, the Millennial Mom turns to technology. She has the choice of thousands of apps that can do everything from ordering birthday gifts to selecting the color of her baby's nursery

## Popular Apps Among Millennial Moms

| Dinner Spinner | MyFitnessPal |
| --- | --- |
| Dropbox | OmniFocus |
| giggle's Best Baby Registry | Parenting Magazine's Ages & Stages |
| Mint | Period Tracker |

# #59 Millennial Moms are stressed but find new outlets for relief.

For the Boomer mom, stress relief was found in aerobics, pedicures and reading a good book in the bathtub, but the Millennial Mom has added new activities to the list. Millennial Moms are more likely to turn to yoga, meditation and crafting for stress management. In our survey, 55% of Millennials say they relieve stress through reading, 39% take a bath and 28% turn to yoga or an organized exercise class.

*"Exercising and essential oils."—Sarah C., 29*

*"Pinterest."—Shannon, 32*

*"Adult coloring books."—Tara J., 29*

*"Zumba and reading."—Victora A., 33*

# #60 It's not enough to be part of a group; she wants to be a contributor.

We've already explored the Millennial Mom's desire to collaborate with brands, but it doesn't stop there. She wants to actively contribute to groups when she's a member. BSM Media assembles Millennial

Moms regularly to be part of brand ambassador programs for clients. When we approach Mom Influencers, one of the first things they want to know is how they can contribute. It's never enough just to be a member; they want to explore opportunities to forge a deeper relationship with the brand. They will suggest content ideas and ways to leverage their network of followers. In some ways, it requires more work and creative thinking on the part of the brand because Millennial Moms want to constantly be engaged. The programs you design around Millennial Moms have to be ever-changing, possibly pushing boundaries to accept consumer-generated content and evolving with the relationship. Marketers who rely on "me-too" marketing and planning sessions that set tactics in stone a year before execution will be challenged by the Millennial Moms. It's time to explore real-time, collaborative marketing tactics in order to successfully connect with Millennials.

## #61  She's used to having her conversations interrupted.

Ask a Boomer mom about the challenges she faced while using the phone with a child in the home and she's likely to tell you that she could never speak on the phone without being interrupted. Perhaps this was a foreshadowing of what would become the norm for the Millennial child (who was doing the interrupting in our Boomer scenario) as they became mothers. Today's Millennial Moms are used to having conversations interrupted. We have all likely seen recent proof of this. A Millennial Mom arrives at a restaurant to have lunch with a girlfriend. She sits down and places her iPhone on the table next to her napkin after giving it one more glance to make sure there are no emails or text messages that need her attention. She begins to chat with her friend while sipping her water. Mid-sentence she hears the buzzing sound of her iPhone indicating a new text message and without hesitation, stops the conversation to look down and respond to her child who needs her to bring the baseball glove he forgot to take to school. Satisfied that she has solved the problem, she looks back up and picks up the conversation where she left off.

# #62 After their mothers, Millennial Moms go to friends more often than the pediatrician.

**29%** of Millennial Moms prefer to consult a friend with parenting questions

**3%** of Millennial Moms prefer to consult their pediatrician with parenting questions

*"While social media has created a need for perfectionism in parenting, it has also created a virtual support system where resources are at our fingertips. The first place I seek parenting advice from is Facebook, Instagram and Twitter. That advice comes from peers and brands on those social channels."—Vanessa C., 32*

# #63 Small blue characters and a purple dinosaur influenced Millennial Moms.

Even though we might cringe at hearing the name, *Barney & Friends* had a tremendous impact on the Millennial generation. The big purple dinosaur ushered in a new standard in children's television. Networks like Nickelodeon and the Disney Channel targeted Millennials with dedicated children's programming. Many shows like *Barney & Friends* focused on straightforward moral lessons and the value of teamwork, all with a super-sweetness that challenged kid TV stalwarts *Sesame Street, Zoom* and others.[4] Barney's simple, strictly child-targeted messaging (with no adult subtexts) became a household favorite along with *The Care Bears* and *The Smurfs* among many similar shows, even if parents could only watch in small doses. As Millennials grew up, not only did they have 24/7 children's shows available, they also had their choice of family shows like *Diff'rent Strokes* and *Full House* presenting diverse and nontraditional families. MTV's reality-show lineup dominated much of the Millennial teen's viewing time.

## Popular Television Shows Among Older Millennial Moms

**Toddlerhood/Preschool**

Barney & Friends
The Care Bears
Mr. Roger's Neighborhood
The Snorkles
The Smurfs
Fraggle Rock

**Early Childhood**

The Fresh Prince of Bel Air
Full House
The Cosby Show
Family Matters
Punky Brewster
A Different World

**Preteen/Teen**

Degrassi
Clarissa Explains It All
All That
Salute Your Shorts
Dawson's Creek
90210

**Young Adulthood**

Charmed
The O.C.
The Bachelor/Bachelorette
The Real World
Road Rules
Laguna Beach

## #64 She is less critical of her body than older generations.

The Millennial Mom is comfortable with her body. There are quite a few pop-culture events that have helped her reach her high level of self-confidence. She's been watching the Dove campaign for "Real Beauty" for many years, along with movies like *Mean Girls* that pointed out the wrongness of judging people based on body images. In addition, celebrities like Mindy Kaling and Kim Kardashian post selfies with no makeup and encourage moms to do the same. Photoshopping is out for Millennial Moms. Touched-up photos like the Glamour Shots of the Baby Boomer generation would never fly with Millennial Moms.

## #TakeNote

When it comes to the images of moms you use in advertising and online, make sure that they represent moms like themselves.

Marketers: #MillennialMoms prefer seeing images of real moms rather than models in advertising. Real is in. Photoshop is out!

## #65 Self-curation is a Millennial trend.

I've mentioned more than once thus far the Millennial Mom's desire for uniqueness and self-expression and hopefully you've seen in my examples her willingness to accept individuals for who they are. These open-minded qualities have set in motion a trend of self-curation: expressing yourself in your physical appearance. Millennial Moms are doing this with a rainbow of new hair colors, body ink and grooming behaviors. According to a 2014 Pew Research Study, three out of four people ages 18 to 34 have tattoos, and more than 50% of them are females. There are plenty of other body trends among Millennials, including the elimination of body hair. My BSM Media team has spent hours debating this particular shift in grooming behaviors and whether it's a fashion trend or a generational norm. The debate continues, but it's my opinion that Millennial men shaving their bodies and women eliminating all private hair is a fashion trend that's being fueled by a Millennial desire to be who they want to be, even if it means changing their physical appearance.

*"The circles I travel in pretty much all have ink. So I think it's just become an accepted way to express yourself with art."* —Sarah, 28

*"I've personally never really thought of my ink as tattoos; it's more an external expression of my internal thoughts and feelings. Like my hair."—Shana, 31*

*"In fact, I'd say Millennials got so used to seeing us with ink they view it just like you view changing your hair. If that makes sense."—Cecily K., 37*

# #66 Selfies . . . do I need to say more?

The selfie has risen to stardom thanks in large part to Millennials. When the staff of the Oxford Dictionary declared "selfie" as the word of the year in 2013, it was just two weeks before the record-breaking Ellen DeGeneres selfie at the Academy Awards. This star-filled selfie was tweeted and retweeted over a million times in just one hour. I recently heard an interview with Taylor Swift who says that she takes more selfies with her fans than she signs autographs.

Replacing the Glamour Shots of the 90s, this new form of photo-taking is so popular with Millennials that they could well be called the Selfie Generation. It puts them in the spotlight just as their parents did when they were growing up and leverages other Millennial qualities such as creativity, love for technology and self-expression.

Millennial Moms, particularly the younger ones, love selfies as much as Swift and DeGeneres do. In fact, more than 27% of this generation of moms take selfies a few times a month and 11% snap their images a few times each week. Twenty-one percent of moms say they take selfies a few times a year. In a Pew Research study, 55% of all Millennials have posted a selfie online.

Why take a selfie? Top responses include "When out doing something fun with friends or family that I want to share," "A memory to remember/share" and "I'm with my children and I want to share a photo of them." The most popular reasons to take a selfie revolve around how she looks: "I like the way I look that day," "I'm wearing a new outfit or jewelry that I want to show" and "When I'm having a particularly good hair and makeup day!"

## #TakeNote

My team at BSM Media has found several ways to leverage the Millennial Mom's love of selfies in marketing campaigns. A shout-out here to ElizaBeth Fincannon for her great work creating retail selfie promotions. The client's goal was to bring awareness of its product to moms while also driving consumers to select retailers. Using social media, ElizaBeth created a promotion that rewarded moms for posting a selfie in front of the product on the shelf. The posts of product selfies were creative, clever and best of all, numerous. It's an initiative that we have replicated several times and one that typically garners 2 to 4 million online impressions.

Never estimate the power of the selfie. Today, BSM Media has formalized this program into a group called SocialSpotters: we send moms into retail locations to take selfies with products. It's a true example of creating a marketing tactic based on consumer behavior. For more information on SocialSpotters, you can visit www.socialspotters.com.

## #67 Millennial Moms are digital storytellers.

Moms have always loved to tell stories. They tell stories about their family, experiences with friends and interactions with strangers, brands and pets. Millennials are using technology to bring those stories to life in ways that photo albums and scrapbooks never did. They're combining digital images with social media platforms and documenting nearly every aspect of their lives. Sharing images online allows the Millennial Mom to tell her story quickly and in a form that's easily shared and connects thoughts in a creative manner. Platforms like Instagram and Tumblr allow Millennial Moms to share experiences without the investment of time in lengthy blog posts. Instagram offers a more intimate community of followers that enables the mom to gain acceptance or approval on ideas, product or experience. It's easy for friends and family to "heart" a photo or leave a short comment in response to her digital story. Technology has allowed her access to easy editing that customizes photos quickly, and the use of video clips, emojis and special effects is easy. Best of all, she can obtain the instant response that a Millennial loves so much. For younger Millennials, Tumblr is the creative outlet of storytelling while older Millennials gravitate to Instagram.

## #TakeNote

As a marketer, you want to communicate in the same language as your customer. Storytelling is a great way to communicate the launch of a new product or provide a sneak peek at this season's designs. Use these platforms for exclusive, behind-the-scene sneak peeks or for demonstrating product. Don't forget that in telling your story that Millennial Moms like to see what's behind the company's flashy website. I suggest including interviews with your factory workers or design team, a brief history of the company or even a virtual tour of your facilities. The more unexpected detail you can add to your company's story, the more interested the mom will be in developing a relationship with you. We saw this last year with Britax, the maker of carseats and strollers. In marketing the quality and safety of their products, they could have listed a whole lot of safety features in an ad. Instead, they included interviews with the product assemblers who take the time to ensure that every latch and buckle works. The videos were distributed through blogs and YouTube and connected with moms because it was an authentic view on safety and product, delivered in a story format.

## #68 Smartphones are the camera of choice.

An overwhelming majority of moms take photos and/or selfies with their smartphones (82%) and share them on social media (only 10% say they use a camera). Facebook ranks highest for photo shares at 70%, followed by 58% of moms who share on Instagram. Twenty-nine percent share images on Twitter and 27% through text messages.

## #69 Millennial Moms love taking photos.

From kids' events to selfies (so they can actually appear on a photo once in a while), more than 64% of Millennial Moms say they take photos at home while 27% take pictures at children's events and activities. Other than photos at home, moms love to capture images from a date night with their partner (42%) or out with friends (38%).

### Popular Photo Apps Among Moms

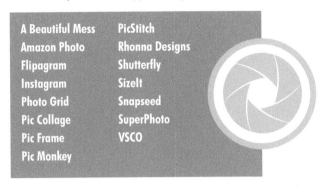

| | |
|---|---|
| A Beautiful Mess | PicStitch |
| Amazon Photo | Rhonna Designs |
| Flipagram | Shutterfly |
| Instagram | SizeIt |
| Photo Grid | Snapseed |
| Pic Collage | SuperPhoto |
| Pic Frame | VSCO |
| Pic Monkey | |

*"The main reason I take pictures are for the memories. I love making Shutterfly books so most pictures I take are used to make the books. I also love to capture God's beauty in nature. Let's be honest, I'm looking for that next Facebook profile picture too."* —Kelly C., 30

*"When I take a picture, it's typically of a moment I want to remember, not a particular thing. I love taking pictures of my daughter, but more than that — of her being totally engrossed in what she's doing. Often times it's of the back of her head while she's admiring something or of her little hands exploring the world around her. Moments I never want to forget. After I take the picture, I love to do a quick edit on Instagram. I don't always pick the filter that best fits the picture but what fits with the moment. Then I love to share it with my friends on social media!"* —Jackie H., 29

*Millennial Moms*

*aren't afraid to*

*try new technology*

*and are quick to adopt*

*if they feel it serves*

*a need for them*

*or their family.*

# CHAPTER
# 3

# Technology

# #70 If technology is the spice of life, then Millennial Moms are hot tamales.

Remember the old adage "The more you have the less you want"? It couldn't be truer than with Millennial Moms. They've never experienced life without computers, so now they gravitate toward times without technology. Unlike the Gen Xers who can remember school without technology, many older Millennials had computer libraries in middle school and younger Millennials were punished for having their cell phones in class. Technology overload seems to be hitting the younger Millennials. Wordless Wednesday on social media and technology-free days are as much a part of the social conversation as constant posts on Facebook and Instagram for the Millennial Mom. They use self-induced restriction from the use of technology. In fact, while Catholic Boomers are giving up chocolate for Lent, Millennial churchgoers gave up Facebook. It's important to remember that it's okay to go silent on technology if done correctly.

## #TakeNote

Speaking the language of Millennial Moms is important and it's okay if the conversation happens without words. Burt's Bees Baby clothing does a great job appealing to the Millennial Mom by posting images of nature to relay information about their 100% organic cotton. Consider posting #Wordless-Wednesday images of your product or related features. Sometimes mimicking the behavior of your target market creates the best relationships; don't be afraid of following their lead.

# #71 She shares with multiple tools.

The Millennial Mom likes to share and she's doing it with many tools, some of which you may find surprising. When it comes to sharing images or information with friends and family members, Facebook is her source of support. Here's the surprise: text messages and email are her second source of support and her most popular sharing tool. Millennial Moms use text messages almost as much as Facebook to share with friends and family. Instagram, Pinterest and Twitter round out the favorites. For European moms (or U.S. moms traveling overseas), WhatsApp is the texting tool of choice.

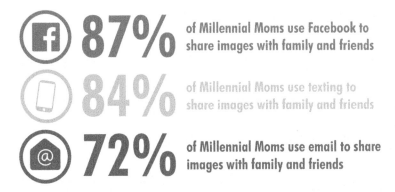

**87%** of Millennial Moms use Facebook to share images with family and friends

**84%** of Millennial Moms use texting to share images with family and friends

**72%** of Millennial Moms use email to share images with family and friends

## #72 Too much information.

Millennials like to post almost every aspect of their life, but 90% of Millennial Moms in the BSM Media survey feel like other people post too much information (TMI) online.

## #73 Millennial Moms sometimes like to be ephemeral or anonymous.

Even the biggest stars want a little alone time and the same goes for the attention-seeking Millennial. The popularity of Snapchat and Yik Yak resonates with younger Millennials who are tomorrow's moms. They have a desire for a space that's safe from broadcasting and/or forwarding to a mass group of followers. Sometimes they don't want to broadcast their news nor do they want to save it. Snapchat is a social media platform that allows the user to send a quick video or photo but only permits it to be viewed once, and in less than 10 seconds. It's the place where a mom can go to send a quick shot of a strange skin rash on her child to her best friend for advice, or share a dress option with a friend. The best part is that it disappears and cannot be saved. It's the anti-Facebook.

Yik Yak is an app that allows you to anonymously post anything you want within a geographical radius. It's a big thing on college campuses where coeds will critique companies, parties and other coeds. Other users agree or disagree on your comments. The best part for younger Millennials is that all comments are anonymous.

Chat apps offer them a rest from all of the public socializing. It gives them a safe haven where they don't have to worry about offending anyone.

## #TakeNote

When seeing a headline that reads "X million Millennials on Snapchat" most marketers begin to salivate over the possibility of pushing out their message to Snapchat viewers. Immediately they put out an email to their agency or social media managers saying they must get their brand on Snapchat without any idea as to what it entails.

Traditional push marketing on chat apps like Snapchat won't work with Millennial Moms. First, they don't want push marketing. Secondly, this is their area of rest. The brands that connect with moms on chat apps will do so through content that is entertaining and offers her escapism. I prefer to use such platforms for social listening since they involve no chatting at all. Sometimes the best marketing is the simple act of listening. Social listening: it's one of the best tools you have in marketing.

3.6 million +
monthly active users

100 million +
monthly active users

Aside from social listening, chat apps do offer brands the opportunity for unique relationships that they can't get anywhere else. Brands like Comedy Central, Sour Patch Kids, Red Bull and Cosmopolitan are all utilizing Snapchat in fun and engaging ways. One of the benefits brands find from a presence

on Snapchat is the development of one-to-one relati
with customers. You can assume that the only people
going to follow a brand in this private space are cor
who want to have a relationship with the brands the
lowing.

# #74 Wearable technology is her bling.

It should come as no surprise that the practical and tech-savvy Millennial Mom has found a way to lose weight while shopping for groceries or toting kids to school. Millennial Moms have fueled the trend of wearable fitness devices. It's not enough for them to wear a Fitbit or something similar, so they create Facebook groups to support their efforts, which they then track on an app. Wearable technology is finding its way into jewelry, baby clothes and even onto the family pet. It's a sign that Millennial Moms accept the idea that technology is an integrated part of their daily lives. It makes you wonder if traditional companies might find ways to externalize their product into wearable technology. For instance, what if an Apple watch could transmit odors and Yankee Candle funded a new way to deliver us scents? Or instead of printing your photos on an HP printer, what if you could project them through a wearable necklace?

# #75 Millennial Moms are early adopters of new media.

Snapchat, Yik Yak, Vine and Periscope are all attracting more Millennials than any other generation. Millennial Moms aren't afraid to try new technology and are quick to adopt if they feel it serves a need for them or their family. A week doesn't go by without another social media platform making headlines in *AdAge* or *PR Week*. With each one, marketers feel that they must quickly learn the ins and outs of the platform and quickly launch an account. Keep in mind, however, that even though Millennial Moms are early adopters of new media, they must first find a purpose for it in their busy lives. This may be why Google+ has seen such slow adoption by moms. It doesn't provide a specific solution for them.

## #TakeNote

Be aware of these new social media platforms, even going so far as to reserve your brand's username. However, it's not necessary to be active on every platform to create meaningful relationships with moms.

## #76 Millennial Moms are adopting Periscope as their newest social media platform.

At the time that this book went to print, Periscope was just launching in the United States. Interestingly, this is one platform that took hold in Europe faster than in the U.S. Perhaps it's because younger millennials have SnapChat but we are seeing older Millennial Moms adopting Periscope at a higher rate. It will be interesting to see how the content of live broadcasting will evolve. Currently, moms are experimenting with short five-minute chats and behind-the-scene footage from special events, while brands are broadcasting from sponsored events. I think the smartest users will begin to broadcast short informational segments with Periscope. For instance, I can envision Travel-ingMom.com broadcasting "City of the Week" each Tuesday at 5 pm and showcasing the flavors, sites and attractions of that city. Or Hampton Inn might broadcast tips for the business traveler every Sunday at 6 pm. Branded scheduled content in very short form is where I see Periscope going in the near future.

## #77 Where's my smartphone?

Half of all moms feel anxious without their smartphone. There's that feeling of dread when they think they might have lost it. Forty-six percent of Millennial Moms report they feel instant anxiety while 7% get a knot in their stomach and another 4% break out in a sweat. In fact, our moms reported everything from twitching fingers to heart palpitations when they don't have their cell phones.

Smartphones are the modern day security blankets for #MillennialMoms who report feeling anxious when they can't find their phones.

**#78** Millennial Moms are on their smartphone an average of 3 – 4 hours per day.

**Time Millennial Moms Spend On Their Phone**

3-4 = 24-28 = 1,248+
hours/day      hours/week      hours/year

**#79** Smartphones are acceptable, wherever and whenever.

Thirty-three percent of Millennials believe it's okay to use their cell phone at a family dinner while 22% approve of using one during a class or lecture, according to a Pew Research Study. Younger Millennial Moms also believe it's okay to sleep with their smartphone and confess to checking it at least once during the night. They love their wireless device so much that it has become an acceptable bathroom companion.

According to BabyCenter.com research, it's very likely that Mom could be shopping at the dinner table: 44% of Millennial Moms have made a purchase from a smartphone in the past week. What all this means is that your customer is omnipresent with a mobile device and could be engaged with your brand anytime or anywhere. It's imperative to convey your message in short, relevant and easy-to-access "sound bytes."

**#80** Millennials use their smartphone in different ways than do older generations.

Although the frequent use of smartphones for texting, emails and calls is similar throughout all generations, Millennial device usage changes in the area of Voice over IP (VoIP) applications and video consumption. Millennials are twice as likely to use their smartphone to watch videos or live events and 1.5 times more likely to use Skype or other VoIP apps, like Vipe.[1]

**#81** Move over, desktops, Millennials access the Internet through their smartphones.

Marketers would do well to heed the call for mobile-friendly solutions for busy moms, 43% of whom use their phones versus home computers to hop on the Internet.[2] Companies with strong mobile applications, like Target and Starbucks, owe their success in part to recognizing what moms want and offering solutions and deals.[3] Mobile coupons are certainly valuable for brands and appreciated by Millennials. Target's Cartwheel app includes deals, timesaving features and a strong Facebook tie-in that lets moms share it all on social media. Starbucks incorporates rewards, payment options and entertainment options with their "Pick of the Week" free song download.

## #TakeNote

An effective, long-term strategy includes elements beyond saving money. Simply look at the five core values of moms (you can find them in the introduction to all of my previous books) to learn how meeting these needs of moms through streamlined, even compact strategies can be priceless in mom engagement.

## #82 Don't call Millennial Moms on the phone.

Over 50% of Millennial Moms say that they spend less than 20% of total use of their mobile phone using it as a phone.

## #83 There's an app for that — maybe even 31 of them on her wireless device.

The average Millennial Mom has 31 apps on her wireless device, although she only uses nine of them on a regular basis. She finds them through friends, recommendations and searching the App Store. When she's determining which apps to buy for her children, she looks for recommendations from other moms and mom groups as well as by online research.

When it comes to gaming for herself, 15% of Millennials say they have five or more gaming apps on their wireless device and another 33% have at least two games, which is considerably higher than the total of the two prior generations. Only one game or no games at all are on their devices, according to 60% of Boomers and Gen Xers.

# #84 If there's an app for that, she'll find it — but she w more than $2 for it.

She's always on the lookout for a timesaving or en app, but she doesn't want to pay more than $2 for it. A to our research, this is the cap for more than 60% of mc you want to dive deeper into her pocket, do it with a ⌐ s app. The same group of Millennial Moms is willing to pay up to $4 if it's an app for their sons or daughters.

# #85 Millennials think these brands are doing a good job engaging with them through mobile applications.

**Brands Millennial Moms Feel Engage Them Well Through Mobile Apps**

# #86 Technology has influenced how the Millennial Mom parents.

According to the 2015 C.S. Mott Children's Hospital National Poll on Children's Health, more than half of mothers say they discuss parenting challenges on social media platforms. Common parenting topics discussed on forums, blogs and social media (such as Facebook) include nutrition and eating tips at 26%, sleep issues at 28% and discipline at 19%. A large majority of these moms — 70% — say that engaging with other parents about relevant topics helps them to not feel alone.

In some ways, the ability to publicly air parenting challenges has created a new type of relationship among mothers. On one hand, the ability to find answers and build camaraderie is helpful but also opens the door to criticism and judgment. Revealing sensitive/embarrassing information or personal location information is seen as a safety threat that's now called "over-sharenting," and is met with swift and harsh criticism by most parents.

*"I definitely think mothers are tougher on each other because of social media. I think moms are quicker to jump to conclusions about other parents based on social media posts rather than knowing the family directly or understanding the whole situation. Some moms use social media as a way to look perfect, only showing the best sides of themselves and their children. This definitely causes other moms to feel inadequate. It is an indirect way that social media is making moms feel less than. I really like seeing moms having real moments with their kids. Good or bad."—Heidi J., 31*

*"I definitely think moms are harder on each other thanks to Facebook. We share everything but tend to forget that everyone has their own way of parenting. I have a child who has severe nut allergies and found a group that I thought would help me learn to help keep him safe. What I found instead was a group of mostly moms who probably started off meaning well, but have adopted a stance of 'nuts are evil and if you even touch them you are wrong.' They went crazy when I mentioned that I let my son sit next to his good friend while he ate a peanut butter sandwich. I was worried and watched the whole time and made sure hands were washed as soon as they finished eating. I was worried about my son and how it would work but I wanted him to be able to enjoy his field trip with his friends and classmates without feeling like the odd child out. Every single mom told me that I made the wrong decision and it was the equivalent of pointing a loaded gun at his head. Personally, I saw it as a chance for him to live life as normal as possible because as he grows older there will be more situations like this and I'm 99 percent sure he'll be able to handle it without any problems."—Jennifer S., 33*

## #TakeNote

Social media gives brands the opportunity to listen to these parenting conversations and react to trends or seasonal topics. This is one of those situations where inserting social listening into your tactics will pay off. Let me give you an example. One of your followers posts that her son is having sneezing fits at school and it's causing him to get sent to the office. You watch as 20-plus moms chime in about their child's sneezing problems in class. It started as a discipline post but now is focused on allergies. So if your product is a children's allergy remedy, this is an opportunity to join the conversation with your solution. It's natural and it's relevant to the mom. *Bingo!* A win-win for all the allergy moms *and* your brand.

We often coach our clients to create a list of words that relate to the solution that their product offers. For example, if you are that allergy brand, then your terms might be "sneezing," "sniffles," "drowsiness" and "allergies." Every morning search those terms with and without a hashtag in front of them. Find out on social media platforms like Twitter and Instagram where mothers are having conversations that are relevant for your brand. They could be your next best customer and marketing tool.

## #87 They are more generous with screen time for their children.

Millennial Moms allow their children more screen time each day than Gen X or Boomer mothers. More than half (60%) of the younger cohort permit up to two hours a day while only 45% of the older moms allow the same amount of screen time. Interestingly, almost 10% of the Gen X and Boomer moms who had children over the age of two said they hadn't allowed their children any screen time, while less than 1% of Millennials noted the same.

#MillennialMoms are more likely to allow their children screen time than other generations.

## #88 Edutainment is her standard for content for her children.

We've already discussed how much Millennials value education. The industry that has felt the desire for education most is perhaps the toy industry. The Millennial Mom wants her children to have fun but she expects them to be learning as well. A

'or this new combination of fun and education
:." Brands such as LeapFrog and Baby Einstein
vay for almost all toy companies to add an edu-
nent to their products. I walk the aisles of the
:ar looking for trends. It's almost as if product
aken their pitch from the same script. They all
start out by telling you about the educational elements of their
toys. Terms like "learning patterns," "reading foundation" and
"multilevel learning" are all part of the product elements.

## #89 Millennials Moms have created prenatal digital dependency.

Once she decides to have a baby, the Millennial Mom has
almost limitless resources for every stage, from conception
through pregnancy and childbirth. Apps cover everything from
ovulation tracking and baby names to stages of pregnancy and
baby registries. Community forums are also popular with this
generation as they seek support, validation and information
from like-minded moms.

These tech-savvy natives have brought digital dependency
to all things motherhood.

## #90 YouTube is the search engine of Millennial Moms.

It's customized television that is instantaneous, shareable,
informative and portable —and over 65% of Millennials interact
with it every week. As the YouTube user base approaches one
billion and YouTube celebrities are more popular than traditional
stars, it's no surprise that moms of all generations watch videos
online at least a few times a week, according to our research.
Nearly 25% of moms said they view videos daily. Both of those
numbers increase when segmenting Millennial Moms in the
data. Twenty-four percent of Millennial Moms watch videos
daily and more than 55% watch video online multiple times a
week.

From watching music videos and makeup tips to life hacks
and daily vlogs, Millennials consume a lot of video content on
YouTube. The easiest way for viewers to stay up-to-date with
new videos from their favorite content creators is by subscribing
to the creators' channels. Millennial Moms find value in YouTube

subscriptions because they provide a convenient, easy, on-demand entertainment library from trusted sources, without a lot of searching. With over 300 hours of videos uploaded to YouTube every minute, finding quality videos that relate to moms' interests can be difficult at times. However, with sites like MomTV.com, moms can easily find videos for and by moms.

Sixty-four percent of Millennial Moms in our survey subscribe to YouTube channels, compared to only 54% of Generation X mothers. When Millennials upload their own videos to YouTube, it's content about their family and special moments. Product reviews are equally as popular. Nearly half of all Millennial Moms who said they upload video point to product reviews as content. Almost 35% of these younger moms upload their own video to YouTube at least once a month.

Knowing the "what" and "how" these young moms are watching can be an important bit of knowledge. In addition to YouTube, it probably won't surprise you that Millennial Moms find the videos they watch via Facebook. On both sites, they enjoy videos that are cute and funny and I've already talked about the popularity of beauty videos with this young cohort. What is very interesting is how many moms watch videos together. They lean in to watch on someone else's mobile device or iPad almost 25% of the time. Sharing videos happens in person as much as it does via Instagram and Twitter. This is all good news for marketers who can easily deliver inspirational, entertaining and authentic content to a group of women who might otherwise be numb to advertising.

Needless to say, YouTube is an important marketing tactic that deserves the attention of brands. Amazon has also seen the power of video review and expanded their "Video Short" content. In fact, when we asked moms where they watch videos outside of YouTube, 86% responded that they watch videos on Amazon. Over half, 55% of these moms, said they expect to see video on a manufacturer site. For marketers, I predict that in the next six to twelve months, brands will shift from blog tours to video tours where they're asking social media Mom Influencers to upload video reviews of their product to sites like YouTube.

I will make another prediction: traditional public relations agencies won't like this shift in tactics because some of these platforms won't produce the millions of online impressions that a Twitter party or blog review can produce. What they won't appreciate is that the numbers won't be large but they will be meaningful and produce sales. Unfortunately, some brands don't measure the success of a traditional social media campaign on sales but rather on impressions, Facebook "likes" and other ambiguous results that only imply sales. A video with a mom praising a product on an Amazon page has to be the most powerful sales tool we've seen in this space in a long time. The possibility of video reviews tied to product on product pages excites me so much that I pursued a partnership with Amazon for my own video portal, MomTV.com. Today you can find MomTV "Mom Review" videos on product pages throughout Amazon.com. It's a powerful tool and we look forward to forging the way in the Mom Market. The best advice for brands right now? If you haven't started shifting some of your marketing budget to video, it's time. Well past time.

## #TakeNote

There are several tactics that I suggest marketers explore to reach moms through video. First, don't be afraid to ask the social media moms and bloggers who you already work with if they do video. Many are migrating over to video and trying their hand at live broadcasting. You can experiment by expanding your request to Mom Bloggers to include a video that you can use on your social media outlets and they can promote through theirs.

Secondly, check out MomTV.com. There are a number of ways that marketers are using this platform, from live events to video review distribution. It's free to upload your own videos as well as the clips you've produced with bloggers. You can also engage in the Amazon video review partnership that exists.

Third, subscribe to some Mom Channels on YouTube to gain a sense of who's producing what in the realm of video.

The "Kid President" is one of my favorite channels. He has million of views and moms love him. Finally, consider teaming up with some of the popular Mom YouTubers. I'll talk about this more in Fact #95.

### Popular YouTube Channels Among Moms

| | |
|---|---|
| Buzzfeed Video | Michelle Phan |
| Convos With My 2-Year-Old | ModernMom |
| Cute Girls Hairstyles | The Ellen Show |
| Daily Davidsons | The Fine Bros |
| Jenna Marbles | The Mom's View |
| Laura in the Kitchen | Shaytards |

## #91 Millennials create videos with smartphones.

Creating videos is second nature to Millennial Moms, particularly with the tech tools available to them. Phones are the most popular video tool, with 46% using iPhone and 40% with Androids to capture video, while 35% use video-capable cameras and 21% record from a tablet. The "old-fashioned" video camera is the tool of choice for 14% of moms. Now they can broadcast from their smartphones with Periscope.

## #92 Videos: they make moms laugh, help her learn and lead her to purchase.

If the old saying goes, "A picture is worth a thousand words," then I would say a video is worth 2,000-plus. Everyone loves to see actual product images and videos that show a product in action, either worn or used by "real" people. Moms are certainly no different. As one mom said, "If a product looks good when photographed by a 'real' person, then I'm more likely to believe in its quality." Eye-catching images attract attention and influence purchasing decisions. "If it catches my eye I am more likely to take a closer look, thus discovering products I may never have noticed before." Another mom says, "Images definitely help with my purchases as it gives me an idea of what I'm looking for."

Millennials will view content produced by brands. Here are a couple of examples of brands that got it right. Similac's "The Mother 'Hood" video became a viral sensation by cleverly pointing to the big issues that divide moms: work, feeding preferences and parenting styles to name a few. In the end, when one mom's child is in danger, the entire playground comes together. This sense of unity and community, clearly the goal with a marketing-campaign title of "Sisterhood of Motherhood," resonated with moms to the tune of 8 million views logged in a very short time. Tempur-Pedic also scored a home run with the Mother's Day launch of the "You're Important — Sleep Like It" campaign targeted at sleep-deprived moms. The surprisingly emotional video offered a much-appreciated "Thank you" while addressing an issue that all moms understand — sleep deprivation — with the brand as the solution.

## #TakeNote

Understanding the where and why of video consumption is important information for brands to consider when engaging with Millennial Moms. Over 44% of moms watch videos that are shared by friends and family on social media, and 35% will search for a brand-produced video when researching a product or service.

## #93 Millennial Mom bloggers are more likely to integrate video into their social media sharing.

If you prefer to look beyond your existing blogger relationships for video, you might consider working with popular YouTube Moms. With the increase in video consumption, the emergence of the YouTubers as spokespersons and content providers has grown. Much like the bloggers of late, marketers are clamoring to engage with the most popular faces on video. I have a few warnings to share should you find yourself on this path. First, beware of the ticket price. Many of the most popular video personalities are requesting very high fees to produce a video for a brand. Whether or not the price tag is warranted is yet to be determined but my suggestion is to look at the overall reach of your potential partner. Recently, I received a proposal for $100,000 for one three-minute video. The network had 400,000 followers on YouTube. Now, you may be saying, "Wow, almost a half million viewers!" But when I looked at their Twitter, Instagram and Pinterest platforms, followers were almost non-existent. If there's one thing you should have as a takeaway from this book, it's that an integrated approach is very important when marketing to Millennial Moms. Don't just throw your money at a YouTuber for the sole objective of doing something new. My guess is that as more and more moms become comfortable in front of the camera, the law of supply and demand will take effect and the price for content creation will fall. Secondly, take a peek at some of their subscribers before you jump up and down at their audience numbers. Recently, I was excited to find a new up-and-comer YouTube Mom only to discover that half of her viewers were Boomer men who happened to like blondes. Something you should also be aware of is the relationship between bloggers and Maker, the large network which manages distribution of some of the biggest YouTubers videos. Many bloggers do not like Maker. The reasons are many and often individual in nature but it's a fact worth noting.

"It is important for bloggers and brands to use video because it helps their audience and customers truly identify and share information easily; not everybody likes to read long paragraphs but rather want information quickly and efficiently. I personally prefer to read but I know many people my age would rather not. Additionally, video adds that personal touch that Millennials crave."—Kathy K., 29

"We, as an audience, want to feel unique and share our opinions and favorite brands; an easy way of doing it is sharing videos that we identify with, making video the perfect vehicle to share a brand's message."—Susan P., 35

"It's almost as if everything we share, as Millennial Moms, tells a story of who we are and what we believe, so it's very important to feel identified with the brand's messages."—Denisse I., 29

# #94 Millennial Moms are as likely to watch Netflix as they are to watch network TV.

Watching their favorite shows has taken on a new look for the Millennial Mom. As many Millennial Moms watch shows on Netflix as do on major networks like CBS, NBC or ABC. Compared to Gen Xers, they are more likely to tune in to Hulu Plus and Amazon Prime to watch TV. In fact, Millennials are more likely to watch their shows on these two platforms than they are on premium channels such as HBO and Showtime.

**What Millennial Moms Are Watching Daily**

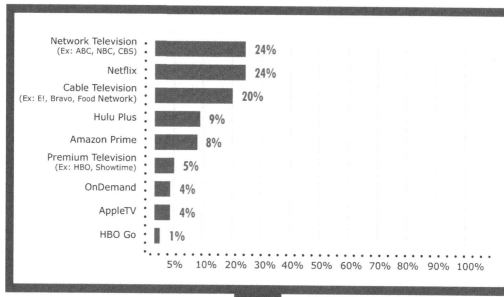

# #95 "Don't bother me, I'm binge-watching."

Escape. It's something that every generation of moms has sought from their chaotic lives. For the Boomer mothers it was reading magazines before bed, while Gen X moms spent time browsing online. For Millennial Moms, it's binge-watching favorite television shows. Gone are the days of anticipating the season-ending cliffhanger. With the rise in popularity of the digital video recorder (DVR) and streaming services like Netflix and Hulu, Millennials have grown accustomed to binge-watching their favorite TV shows. Millennials are no longer confined to watching one episode of a TV show on a certain night at a certain time each week. Instead, they watch TV when it fits into their schedules, often watching between 2 – 6 episodes consecutively on a variety of devices. Binge-watching allows viewers to stay caught up on current TV shows and deeply connect with the characters and plot lines, creating what they describe as a more enjoyable and fulfilling viewing experience. I think Grant McCracken, a cultural anthropologist, best explained the emergence of binge-watching. He describes the need for long narrative in a world where expression of thought has been reduced to 140 characters. He goes on to explain in his white paper that TV is no longer a time to zone out, but for Millennials to tune in. They schedule TV time and make time for viewing regardless of the delivery device. TV viewing is purposeful.

## #96 Millennials and music.

For decades, music has been a defining generational characteristic. For Millennial Moms, it may be *how* they listen to music rather than what they are listening to specifically. The most common delivery device for tunes is their smartphone, followed by their computer and television. Yes, television. Almost half of the Millennial Moms in our research indicated that they listen to music through their television. Generation X mothers are more likely to use an iPod or MP3 player or stereo for music. When it comes to obtaining music, Millennial Moms are more likely to use Pandora, Spotify and YouTube than the general sampling of mothers. Pandora is the number-one source for Millennial Moms, edging out iTunes. So the next time you want to add music to a Millennial party, expect to hear it piped in through a smartphone. According to a recent report about on-demand music streaming by age, 54% of Millennials have downloaded more than 30 songs in the last month.[4]

*The influence of Millennial Moms covers a myriad of subjects, with the most popular being parenting and education.*

# CHAPTER
# 4

## Influence

# #97 Mother knows best.

As marketers, one the most important nuts to crack regarding any consumer is about who and what influences their behaviors. These influences may include purchasing decisions, parenting styles and lifestyle, among many others. Respect for the opinions of family and friends of Millennial Moms translates into influence. Interestingly, Gen Xers rank friends as the greatest influencer. However, there is a slight difference between Generation X and Millennials on this subject. Generation X moms put more credence in the recommendations of friends rather than family. This may be the result of the high number of Gen Xers who were raised in split households and the lack of helicopter parents in their life. The Millennials became dependent on their parents at a young age and that dependency was maintained well after college. It should be of little surprise that the level of influence remains as they become mothers.

### People Who Influence Millennial Moms

| | |
|---|---|
| Family . . . . . . . . . . . . . . . . 48% | Clergy . . . . . . . . . . . . . . . 2% |
| Friends . . . . . . . . . . . . . . . 27% | Colleagues . . . . . . . . . . . . <1% |
| Other Moms . . . . . . . . . . . 11% | Educators . . . . . . . . . . . . . <1% |
| Doctors/Medical Prof . . . . . 7% | Other Professionals . . . . . . . <1% |
| Brands . . . . . . . . . . . . . . . 2% | The Media . . . . . . . . . . . . . <1% |
| Celebrities . . . . . . . . . . . . 2% | |

# #98 Save your money — celebrities don't resonate.

"Is it worth spending money on a celebrity endorsement?" This is one of the most frequent questions I receive from companies. From the Boomer generation through the Gen X population to today's Millennial Moms, my answer has been "Probably not." Some people take my advice and others decide to throw thousands of marketing dollars at a B-list celebrity to endorse their product. Finally, I welcome a generation of mothers that emphatically supports me on this topic. Forty-seven percent of Millennial Moms are least likely to purchase a product based on a celebrity endorsement. In fact, less than 6% said they are more likely to pull out their wallet for a product endorsed by a celebrity. *AdWeek* concurred in August 2014 in an infographic on Millennials: 68% are completely unfazed by celebrity endorsements or star-studded ads. The good news for marketers is that you can save or reallocate your marketing budget to other areas and most likely achieve a higher return on investment.

 **47%** of Millennial Moms reported that they are LEAST LIKELY to purchase a product endorsed by a celebrity

## #TakeNote

YouTube personalities and high-profile social media influencers can provide an effective alternative to celebrity endorsements. Before they were mothers, many of the Millennial Mom YouTubers attracted audiences to their video channels and today enjoy popularity among growing online audiences. Several brands such as T.J.Maxx, Dove and McDonald's have effectively used high-profile social media influencers to draw Millennial Moms to their brand. The best way to identify the cybermom who best fits your brand is to look at the subscribers to the social media channels. If you can identify your target market in her subscribers and her content aligns with the values of your brand, she's your gal. You can utilize her in the same way you would engage with a celebrity spokesperson but at a fraction of the price. Following are a few names you should consider, although some may not be Millennials — nor do they need to be. Their appeal crosses generations.

## Mom Influencers and Where they Live Online

| | | |
|---|---|---|
| **Maria Bailey**<br>MomTalkRadio.com & MomTV.com | **Heather Mann**<br>DollarStoreCrafts.com | **Jessica Shyba**<br>MommasGoneCity.com |
| **Amy Bellgardt**<br>MomSpark.net | **Amy Mascott**<br>TeachMama.com | **Danielle Smith**<br>ExtraordinaryMommy.com |
| **Beth Blecherman**<br>TechMamas.com | **Audrey McClelland**<br>MomGenerations.com | **Vera Sweeney**<br>LadyAndTheBlog.com |
| **Kathy Cano-Murillo**<br>CraftyChica.com | **Jessica McFadden**<br>AParentInAmerica.com | **Sara Wellensiek**<br>MomEndeavors.com |
| **Natalie Diaz**<br>Twiniversity.com | **Colleen Padilla**<br>ClassyMommy.com | **Ilana Wiles**<br>MommyShorts.com |

## #99 The Millennial Mom believes she is an influencer online and offline.

"How many moms a year do you feel you truly influence online?" This is the question we posed to our pool of Millennial Moms. More than 40% responded that they influenced over 500 people a year. Twenty-five percent of these women said they influence more than 500 others in a one-month span, while 13% said they influenced the same number — 500 — weekly. The influence of these women takes place offline as well.

The influence of Millennial Moms covers a myriad of subjects, with the most popular being parenting and education. Over 40% of Millennial Moms believe they influence other moms in the categories of cooking, saving money and crafting. Marketers in these categories or with products that can be used in any of these areas should be engaging with Millennials to help spread their messages.

Millennials Moms believe their friends and family view them as an influencer because of their personal character and online behaviors. Many point to their honesty and good intentions as the main reasons others ask for advice on products and services. However, their actions online seem to establish their credibility as an influencer as well. Many credit the intense research they perform online as well as their exposure to new products through their blogs and social media platforms.

The Generation X mom is more likely than Millennials to influence her friends on deals, travel and healthy living. Technology ranks moderately in both generations.

*"I do view myself as an influencer, but not more than a friend in 'real life.' I love sharing inspiration and helping even one person with a new idea or product they hadn't seen or tried before. I feel helpful and useful when someone is able to save time, money or be inspired by a product or idea I share."—Allison W., 31*

*"I know what my social group and readers want, like and need. I know that they are as super-interested in what I have to say as I am in what they have to say. When I promote something, it's easy to see that I'm an influencer based on affiliate links where they are purchasing what it is that I'm promoting and the cash incentives that I'm collecting monthly."—Courtney V., 25*

*"My sharing with other moms — whether that be a new product, idea, or a learning experience in the form of a workshop or conference — comes from a deep-rooted passion for support and community amongst other women. Influence is a funny thing because I think that at the root of it, I have created an authentic connection to others with my own life (relatable or otherwise) whether it be imperfections, experiences or lifestyle."—Nadia C., 33*

*"I blog about deals because I know how much of an impact using deals and coupons has made on my family. It's allowed us to use the money we save for other things in our lives, including vacations, emergency fund, and saving for the future. It makes me happy to provide a resource for moms to save money and time because I've done some of the work for them to put money back in their wallets."—Maria R., 30*

# #100 Millennial Moms are connected online but they enjoy face-to-face encounters, too.

Their communities are online and offline. This is a very important concept for marketers and one that is often overlooked in planning tactics. So much attention is given to the power of social media that marketers often forget that moms still enjoy the sense of community offline as well. Millennial

Moms belong to local groups such as Stroller Strides, a meetup group in which new moms will exercise with other moms and their babies. Meeting in parks and playgrounds, groups like Stroller Strides give moms the opportunity to develop friendships and engage in the non-digital world.

To fully understand how much moms enjoy face-to-face interactions, I invite you to stand in the lobby of a blogger conference to hear just how much Social Media Moms love to meet their peers in the flesh. It's hard to miss the exuberant greetings when they identify a mother they've known only via Twitter or Facebook. Millennial Moms enjoy interacting offline with fellow mothers, just as they do online. The average Millennial Mom belongs to three offline groups. Additionally, Millennial Moms are more likely than their Generation X or Boomer predecessors to attend a moms' night out with girlfriends when they were at the same age.

One way brands can leverage the influence of #MillennialMoms is by sponsoring opportunities for these moms to gather together offline.

## #TakeNote

The opportunity for marketers here is to leverage the offline network a Millennial Mom has while also engaging her online. A common mistake for brands is to select Mom Influencers based solely on their social media reach. They spend significant amounts of money to develop a relationship with the Millennial Mom online but never explore the channels of communication she has with other moms offline. Let's examine a common marketing tactic in blogger outreach. Typically, an agency or brand manager will send a product sample or coupon to a Mom Blogger and ask her to post about it. However, a more efficient tactic would be to not only send her a product to review for her blog, but also send coupons to distribute to other moms at the park or at a classroom event. It's a marketer's dream: one relationship with multiple channels.

At BSM, we'll often engage with bloggers during a campaign by asking them about offline events they're participating in and leverage them. Recently, for a tween-oriented toy company, we identified Mom Bloggers with tweens who might be hosting a slumber party and we seeded the slumber parties with the product. For a client launching a new, high-ticket product, we identified moms who were involved in hosting school auctions and raffles. It's a great way to get your product in front of a lot of moms at once.

# #101 Sharing is her new form of socializing.

For marketers, it's important to understand what motivates a Millennial Mom to share. Overwhelmingly, 67% of Millennial Moms see sharing with other moms as a way to connect and inform. Most of these moms see the act of sharing as a form of socializing. In fact, 38% of moms said that they share as a way to entertain other moms.

Knowing what motivates her to share can go a long way in designing your social media communication calendar. Based on our research, it seems that brands should post information they want shared among customers to be entertaining or informative. Consider creating a funny video showing moms using your product the wrong way — it's not the typical branding approach, but it can be very effective. Brands may also want to create a bond with their target audience. A good example of this is the 2015 Mother's Day video by Pandora. In the video, blindfolded children identify their mothers through the sense of touch. It's a tearjerker that was shared over one million times by moms because they could relate to the emotions shared in the video.

 #MillennialMoms love to share. Developing heart warming or informative content will result in more social shares for your brand.

# #102 Millennial Moms share products they like online.

When moms like a product or service they will share the good news far and wide. In fact, more than 52% of Millennial Moms say they post an online review when a product "exceeds" expectations and 29% when it "meets" expectations. It's interesting to note that barely 18% say they post when a product fails to meet expectations. Moms want to talk about their success in finding great products.

#MillennialMoms respect brands that have responsive customer service teams on social media, review sites, and through private methods.

The primary motivation for posting online reviews is the need to share information, with the main reason being that 61% of moms are "wanting to share [their] experience with other consumers." Another 27% say they post online reviews because these reviews play an important role in their own purchasing decisions.

## #TakeNote

Millennial Moms want to know that your brand cares about her opinion and most particularly the one she posts online. It's important to monitor your online reviews whether they are on Amazon.com, Target.com, Walmart.com or forums on mom-oriented sites. Remember that reviews can also be given on social media channels. I typically recommend to clients that they assign someone to check a select list of review sites every morning and respond accordingly. In the days before brands were comfortable with social media, I would receive numerous calls about whether or not to respond publicly to a complaint about your product. My response is the same today as it was a few years ago: moms are having the conversation with or without you. It's much better to be a part of the discussion than to watch it from the sideline. Today's Millennial wants you to react. It's a sign of respect, so I say go for it. Be yourself. Be honest and be transparent. Thank them for their thoughts and arrange to make amends in a private email or direct messaging if resolution is necessary. Other Millennial Moms will see your response and respect you as a brand for being attentive to your customers. In the end, your

response will generate a multiplier effect for your brand. Here are a few easy ways to demonstrate that your brand cares about its online opinions:
- Respond to reviews
- Acknowledge social media mentions
- Retweet her opinions and comments
- Thank her for the time it took to write a review
- "Like" her posts
- Don't correct her mistakes, whether it's a lack of knowledge of the product or typos in her review

# #103 "Social" is a word with many definitions.

"Social" takes on many different meanings depending on whether you are a marketer, an older Millennial or a younger Millennial. We all seem to adopt a blended definition when interacting with each other. In our research at BSM we decided to ask moms for their definition, confident that understanding this could shed some light on how to create more meaningful engagements. I thought it was interesting that older Millennial Moms included the platform or technology that they used in socializing, while the younger Millennials focused on the interaction without mention of where and how. It certainly shows how the use of technology is so ingrained into the behavior of these younger Millennials that they don't even think about mentioning it. It's almost as if it's presumed that one would use online communities to socialize. In short, it's become second nature to them.

*"'Social' to me means interacting with other people, whether it be in person or online."*—Becky F., 36

*"Being talkative and friendly with anyone on social (media): open for everyone to see in different forms of media . . . example: TV, radio, computer, etc."*—Meg D., 34

*"Relationships."*—Megan M., 22

*"Communicating with friends and strangers."*—Meghan B., 24

# #104 Social media gives marketers insight into the Millennial Mom.

Consider this the formula to understand Millennial Moms on social media: Facebook is what she's doing and where she is, Pinterest is who she wants to be and what she dreams of doing, Instagram is what she's proud of and YouTube is what she wants to showcase.

# #105 Sharing (and spying) is all part of the Facebook experience for Millennial Moms.

Facebook serves a lot purposes for Millennial Moms. Eighty-five percent of these mothers use Facebook to stay connected with friends; however, at least 15% of them confess to using it to stalk old friends. Eighty-five percent of Millennial Moms belong to a private Facebook group. An important note for brands is that 62% of moms say they use Facebook to engage with brands or companies. As I've discussed earlier, they are looking for exclusive deals and coupons. About 15% of Millennial Moms use Facebook to vent when something upsets them. Conversely, 20% use the platform to create a positive online image. Perhaps the most useful behavior for marketers to consider about Facebook has to do with photos. Almost 70% of Millennial Moms say they use it for sharing photos, which presents a valuable marketing opportunity.

## #TakeNote

The best marketing tactics are ones that leverage a commonly known behavior of your consumer. In this case, the behavior is sharing photos on Facebook. There are two ways to approach this. First, use your brand's Facebook page to post photos that inspire or entertain. I talked earlier about #TBT photos being effective, but think beyond just product pictures. If your photos strike a chord with Millennial Moms, then they are likely to share them with friends and family. The second strategy is to invite moms to share their own photos on your Facebook page. This works well, particularly if you have a product that she uses to produce something, such as a meal or craft. Photos, moms and Facebook equal a good recipe for success. An overwhelming number of Millennial Moms want to be able to write on your wall; it's part of the authentic and transparent relationship they want with you.

# #106 Millennial Moms expect brands to show photos of product and include thought-starters on Facebook.

While we're talking about photos, let's explore what moms expect from brands on their Facebook page. Not surprisingly, 75% of Millennial Moms expect to see photos followed by contests and promotions. This is important and easily executable. Moms want photos, contests and discount codes. But it's not all money and status updates that they enjoy seeing on your pages. One-third of Millennial Moms enjoy fun facts about your products while 16% enjoy thought-starters.

# #107 Millennial Moms follow brands on Facebook but they buy from Pinterest.

According to the Center for Marketing Research at the University of Massachusetts, more Millennials follow brands on Facebook over other social media platforms. However, they are more likely to purchase a product based on a pin on Pinterest. Sixty-two percent of Millennials surveyed reported they followed a brand on Facebook, while only 11% pinned a brand on Pinterest. It has been widely documented that moms, regardless of their generation, follow a brand on Facebook for exclusive deals and coupons. Moms use Pinterest in a very different way. Millennial Moms in particular search Pinterest for unique ideas and creative products that are tied to a specific need or solution.

Marketers need to remember that when creating pins or boards, moms often use your product in different ways and for multiple occasions. For instance, the maker of Ball mason jars might be inclined to only create boards on Pinterest that highlight canning fruits and vegetables. However, a quick search on Pinterest will reveal different uses like "Mason Jar Crafts," "Mason Jar Wedding Favors," "Mason Jar Picture Displays" and thousands of other uses for mason jars. Don't limit your use of Pinterest to the traditional ways your company intends the product to be used or you'll miss opportunities for consumer engagement. Imagine the incremental sales your brand can have by the mom who's on Pinterest searching for party favors and falls in love with . . . mason jars used as party favors. Suddenly, you've found "accidental" consumers; this can drive sales growth. Think of Pinterest as an inspiration hub. It's a place to inspire consumers to interact with your product rather than pitching a consumer to buy your product. The relationship is far more meaningful for the consumer, but still allows you to add to your bottom line.

In the same University of Massachusetts study on Millennials, respondents estimated an average amount they spent on social media platforms such as Facebook, Twitter and Pinterest. Although high at $105, Facebook purchases were trumped by Pinterest where Millennials reported they spent $150 on average. Twitter purchases lagged behind both Facebook and Pinterest with an average of $72. The trend uncovered by the university's study was validated in another study by Monetrate which examined all generations of social media users. The Monetrate study showed the average spend from Pinterest was still the highest at $81, compared to $71 on Facebook and $70 on Twitter.

My advice to marketers: get on Pinterest!

# #108 Millennial Moms love Instagram.

Moms post images on Instagram for much the same reasons they do almost everything: to share with others. Whether it's directed at friends, family or followers, 62% of moms say they post because "It's a particularly good picture that I want to share," and 56% say, "It's an experience that I want to share with my friends and followers." Over 31% say they like to go back and look at old photos and 28% enjoy using the photo filters and effects. Instagram won the hearts of moms because it offers easy editing and doesn't require long descriptions like those a user may feel compelled to write with a Facebook post. Older Millennial Moms outnumber younger Millennial Moms on Instagram but the platform serves as a great place to connect with all Millennial Moms.

# #109 Moms blog because it makes them feel connected.

*"For me my blog has always been a ministry! It's not just about saving money on a deal here and there, it's about giving people actual tools that can change their whole life and continue to help them for the rest of their lives! They can then pass on the skills to their children. It makes me happy to know that I'm making a difference in people's lives and I find joy in giving back to others! I never knew in a million years that my now full-time job would be about helping others! I feel so blessed!"—Michelle G.*

*"To be heard, to express myself, to entertain and to make a difference in someone else's life."—Jennifer G., 36*

*"The blog has given me an outlet to share stories and allows me to no longer feel like I'm consistently talking to myself."—Angele L., 32*

# #110 Blogs influence Millennial Moms on all things fashion and beauty.

When it comes to fashion and beauty, blogs are a go-to for Millennial women. Fashion blogs are a top-rated resource when shopping for cosmetics, special event attire, accessories and new fashion trends, according to a study by Edison and Netbase. Thirty percent of Millennials find inspiration for casual clothing from Facebook, while 25% go to Pinterest for accessories and jewelry suggestions. Instagram ranks high in influencing cosmetic purchases. The study also drilled down on social shopping, a growing trend with this generation, with 28% of women saying they are influenced by brands and products that friends and family use and talk about on social media.[1]

#MillennialMoms are making purchases after being inspired by product photos & videos shared on sites like Instagram, Pinterest, and YouTube.

## #TakeNote

This is an area where a company's involvement in social media should have two strategies. The first and most obvious is to create a presence on social media to give followers exclusive looks at new products, colors or styles. Second and equally important, fashion and beauty brands should use social media to learn from their consumers. Pinterest gives brands the opportunity to watch moms who are repinning their products, and YouTube allows them to see how customers are presenting the brand to their peers through the videos they create. You may discover that a YouTuber tells your story better than you do. Social media is a rich landscape of consumer insights and the marketer who doesn't participate in social listening is steering the ship wearing a blindfold.

## #111 Brands validate Moms as influencers.

I am asked often why moms are willing to host in-home parties or to write blog posts about new products without monetary compensation. The answer is simple: it offers validation.

*"Brands validate me as an influencer by understanding me. I'm hyper-connected and consume content on multiple platforms and devices every day. I'm enthusiastic and honest and I like being in charge of the conversations on my site, especially when they appreciate and respect that I feel validated. Brands that know what my blog is about and recognize that I can help promote their products to my target audience and allow me to be honest and sincere about their products make me feel as if I'm not just an influencer, but an effective influencer as well."—Courtney V., 28*

*"I feel that I am an influencer because I have a platform and an audience who is engaged in the topics I'm passionate about. On my platform I was influencing my audience on brands before the brands were involved in the conversation. In the beginning, if I liked something I shared it. There was nothing sponsored, nothing to gain by sharing except the feeling that I may have helped another person. As the digital space has evolved and my platform and audience have grown, brands are now part of the equation. Brands want to use my platform to get out the message about their products.*

*In a way it validates me because I feel I've done something right and that I've built something good that they want to tap into."—*
Kristin C., 34

## #TakeNote

To leverage validation as a motivator, create marketing tactics that elevate the mom among her friends and family. Let me use my own party company, MommyParties.com, as an example. MommyParties are in-home themed parties that influential moms host in their homes on behalf of brands. The brand produces a party box for the moms that's filled with samples, coupons and party activities themed around the products. Recently LeapFrog sponsored LeapTV parties. The moms received a box with a LeapTV, a party agenda, recipes for snacks and games for guests to play. The mom hostess is screened to assure the client that she has an elevated scope of influence. She commits to hosting her party and inviting at least 10 of her friends. There's work involved; that's why the companies ask me about her motivation. She does it because it shows her friends that a major brand believes in her influence and respects what she is doing as a blogger, social media influencer or community leader. It validates her.

There are other ways to validate a mom. Licensing her content for your website validates her ability as a writer. Repinning her craft ideas with your product validates her talents, and providing her a preview of your products validates her professionally. Develop marketing tactics that validate Millennial Moms and you will establish a long relationship with these influencers.

# #112 Follow a Millennial Mom to create excitement.

Nothing excites a Millennial Mom more than having a brand she likes follow her back on Twitter, Instagram or Pinterest or other relevant social networks. It's a good tactic, as shown by the emotions moms describe when a brand follows back: "happy," "connected," "important" and "proud." Relationships are important to a mom, and this is just another sign that you as a brand can confirm to her that it works both ways.

☺ **86%** of moms reported feeling excited or happy when followed by a brand

## #113 Millennial Moms want to work with brands.

Millennial Moms want to partner with brands, particularly if they've built an online persona. For the Millennial Mom this persona can be as a blogger or YouTuber or through one of the many social media platforms. I thought it would be beneficial to ask these moms seeking brand relationships how they feel it's best to leverage their influence.

The majority of Millennial Moms said that providing them with product samples or coupons they can share is the most effective way to benefit from their influence. Fifty-four percent said that engaging them as brand ambassadors is another effective way; see Fact #112 for more in-depth information about brand ambassador programs. I am finding through my own work with brands that ambassadors are providing the best return on investment in terms of social outreach and buzz generation. The authenticity of their reviews cannot be duplicated with other marketing initiatives.

Most moms will tell you that they want to be paid for their efforts, which is a contentious topic I will leave for the social media conferences. I can tell you that there are arguments on both sides that make sense. However, I can also assure you that there are plenty of effective Mom Marketing initiatives that integrate social media–savvy mothers that don't involve pay for placement. I've presented some of them throughout the tips in this book. At the end of the day, I think the most important thing for brands to remember when working with moms is that the relationship needs to be sincere and mutually beneficial. If you believe that paying bloggers somehow discredits a product review, then find moms whose passion for your product is so great that the association with your brand is enough to make them happy. Those moms are out there — you just have to look. I'll say it again: start with social listening.

*"A brand can leverage my influence by giving me creative freedom. Part of the reason people are influenced by my ideas or favorite products is that they trust my thought process and my creativity and they want to hear the different ways or reasons I would use a new product."*—Allison W., 28

*"Brands need to understand the difference between my role as a consumer and my role as an influencer. Using my influence to support a brand is an endorsement many of us take seriously and as a result, our followers expect us to be somewhat of an expert. It's not enough to simply say we like a brand. We need to bring a unique perspective through a unique experience and interaction with the brand."*—Fadra N., 35

## #114 Millennial Moms want to show love to their favorite brands.

I touched on the effectiveness of brand ambassadors in the previous fact. Millennial Moms have their favorite brands and for those they love, they want to help shape them. In fact, only 3% of the Millennial Moms we surveyed said they had no interest in being a brand ambassador for their favorite brand. The top reason for wanting to be part of such a group is the desire to share their knowledge about the brand with others. The sense of community with other people who also love the brand is a motivator as well. This can be seen by the number of fans who "like" product pages on Facebook.

Finding friends with shared interests is something Millennials enjoy. This explains why Red Bull has over 42 million followers and Nutella has almost 30 million. It's fun to share your love for a product with other fun-loving followers. It also unleashes some friendly competition among self-proclaimed consumer experts, which is a marketing opportunity for many brands. Brand ambassadors enjoy receiving coupons, discounts and exclusive information about future products. It's more than just fans helping brands spread their message. Many of the brands BSM Media works with in managing their ambassador programs use the group for insights and research as well. Moms like this aspect. Almost 60% of Millennial Moms see the opportunity to contribute to the brand as a key benefit in being a brand ambassador.

BSM Media is proud to have launched HP's Smart Mom Panel and Chick-fil-A's Mom Panel. Both companies use the groups to shorten the turnaround time on receiving insights and product feedback. In turn, the moms receive product launch information, coupons to share with friends and family and the ability to contribute content for the brand. The groups not only reduce research expenses, but also produce millions of online impressions. There is a significant amount of innovative Mom Marketing taking place in the brand ambassador space. I see it as the best long-term solution to connecting with moms. I do need to mention, however, that I have seen several brands commission their traditional PR firm to create a Mom Panel or brand ambassador program and I cringe at the outcome.

It's important to distinguish between ambassadorships and brand evangelists. The latter are individuals with influence who are engaged and often hired to talk about your brand. Without giving names, let me give you an example. Last year I was asked by a respected PR firm to be an ambassador for a certain brand. They told me I was being selected because of my influence. That was their first mistake. Ambassadors raise their hand to participate because of their undying love for the brand. They aren't selected solely for their influence. Ambassadors have a combination of brand passion and influence to share it. I accepted the position because I liked the brand and my kids used to play with the product, so I figured I could intelligently speak about it in social circles. Then I never heard anything. No email outlining their expectations. No community to join so I could socialize with other moms who also liked the brand. Nothing. That was their second mistake. Ambassador programs should have a community where people can congregate online and share thoughts about the product. Fast forward a year: I've received three pieces of product and a letter each time asking me to go crazy on social media spreading the news about their new toy. That was their third mistake. If I were properly selected as an ambassador, you wouldn't have to ask me to tweet or post; I would do it naturally because I couldn't contain my excitement and love for the brand. My point is that the program was not an ambassador program, but an outreach campaign or evangelist program at best. Everyone likes to launch the newest and hottest initiative, but make sure you or your agency know the ins and outs of an ambassador program. My only other warning about this type of program is the cost. It's not a one-time, once-and-done type of program. It's a relationship-based marketing initiative. This means that you and the moms involved commit to a long-term relationship. You have to be willing to fund it for several years, even if you decide to reselect the moms who participate annually. I could write an entire book on ambassador programs, but the page count would prohibit it. Feel free to reach out to me anytime to answer specific questions. My contact information is included in this book for that reason.

# #115 Millennial Moms won't buy products without reading reviews.

Call it peer pressure on steroids, but Millennial Moms like to know what other moms, who are like them, think about your product. In fact, 32% of Millennial Moms won't buy a product without reading a review. This includes merchandise they purchase offline as well. Although Gen Xers read reviews as frequently as Millennials, they are less likely to let a review prevent a purchase. Interestingly, reviews of complete strangers carry more weight than those produced by the manufacturer. In a recent survey by the Center for Generational Kinetics, 51% of Millennials trust user-generated reviews from blogs and social media over brand content on a company website. Millennial Moms find credibility in reviews that contain a lot of details and when the review gives both pros and cons to the product.

# #TakeNote

It's safe to say that if the Millennial Mom is your target, product reviews should be part of your marketing strategy and they should be found in a number of places online. My suggestion is that brands should focus on making certain that positive reviews are available on Amazon, your website, YouTube and on other shopping sites. Amazon is particularly important as the top review resource for Millennial Moms. Over 85% of Millennial Moms seek out online product reviews on Amazon. Even if they ultimately purchase the product through a different source, they will conduct product research on Amazon.com. Keep in mind that a review doesn't have to utilize a lot of words. Photos posted by friends with a caption that reads "Love this" is as good as a paragraph-long review of your product.

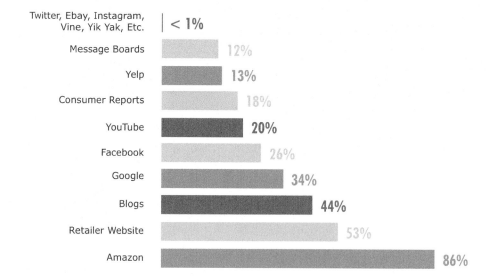

**Where Millennial Moms Seek Out Online Reviews**

| | |
|---|---|
| Twitter, Ebay, Instagram, Vine, Yik Yak, Etc. | < 1% |
| Message Boards | 12% |
| Yelp | 13% |
| Consumer Reports | 18% |
| YouTube | 20% |
| Facebook | 26% |
| Google | 34% |
| Blogs | 44% |
| Retailer Website | 53% |
| Amazon | 86% |

*"I always ask friends, see reviews on Facebook and read blogs. I don't generally trust online reviews at places such as the store you buy the product from, because I feel like the company has control of what is said. It might not be honest."*—Carolyn B., 35

*"When it comes to online shopping I specifically look at reviews from other mothers. Other mothers share my perspective and look at products through the lens of their child. It's a different way of looking at quality and how well a product works in the real world, with a real child. I try to read as many reviews as possible, from the product's website and other sites that sell the same product. I can be influenced by email or Facebook if it comes from one of my friends, or at the least another mother. I look specifically for the reviews that talk about a specific child, with details like age or a name, that way I know that person is a real mother and is looking out for the best interest of her own child."*—Kelly A., 30

### Moms Prefer to Read Reviews Prior to Purchasing These Items

| | | |
|---|---|---|
| Appliances | Children's Toys | Hotel/Vacation Rentals |
| Automobiles | Clothing/Shoes | Jewelry |
| Baby Gear | Electronics | Salon/Spa Services |
| Beauty Products | Furniture | Vitamins/Supplements |

*"I generally read all kinds of reviews to get a good range of opinions. I find it best to read as much as possible to see what the overall opinion is, not just the opinion of one person. There are a lot of people in our neighborhood that post things on Facebook that they enjoy. I can also ask questions if I am looking for a review on something. Other than that, I try to look at the reviews posted on store websites or Amazon. At times I have looked at* Consumer Reports *when making larger purchases or things for the kids (i.e. car seats & strollers). I tend to trust mom reviews the most. They seem to be the most practical and to the point. I don't have a lot of time to look around, so hearing from another mom tends to be the most helpful. Sometimes I worry that the businesses are posting*

*their own reviews to talk up a product. I can be an impulse buyer so if I see an ad on Facebook or email that catches my eye I will look into it. I spend most of my time on email or Facebook, so it is the best form of advertising for me. However, it tends to cause me to purchase things I do not need! Since the ads on Facebook are geared towards things I have liked or shared, they usually pertain to me. The same goes for email — a lot of the ads are for stores I usually shop at anyway. If I see an email advertising a good sale, I try to jump on it."—Colleen C., 29*

# CHAPTER
## 5

# Employment and Work

# #116 Work takes on a new definition.

As they have done with most aspects of life, Millennials have put their own mark on defining work. They are entrepreneurial in spirit, mostly because they seek employment on their own terms. Millennials are confident in their skills and enjoy being creative. Being an entrepreneur allows them to control their own destiny and provides a sense of security. Isn't it ironic that previous generations saw a lifelong corporate job as security and these young people see the risks of entrepreneurship and startups as security? Watching her mom crash through a glass ceiling at work shaped her attitude about jobs and careers. She prefers to work in teams or at least collaborate with others in business. She learns what she doesn't know by networking with other moms online and isn't afraid to tackle tasks in which she has no direct experience.

Older Millennial Moms are more likely to be earning some kind of income even if she is at home with children. Younger Millennial Moms who choose to stay at home with their children have intentions to earn income sometime in the near future. These are women who are creative and confident in utilizing technology to find work-life integration. Notice I didn't say "work-life balance" — Millennial Moms don't seek balance in the same way as their parents did. They believe they can have it all without the Superwoman cape and on their own terms.

# #117 No more Mommy Wars.

It's time to banish two distinguishing terms from our vocabulary: "working mom" and "stay-at-home mom." We asked Millennial Moms who earn income at home to classify their work status. Interestingly, the exact same percentage of mothers claimed the title of Stay-at-Home Mom as Work-at-Home Mom, with another 10% taking on the title of Working Mother. My point is that if you are a company who is still dividing moms into two segments, you are using outdated terms that do not sync with the terms Millennial Moms are using. At BSM Media we tend to use four terms. "In-home mothers" are moms who are in the home and generate no income. "Work-at-home mothers" and "working mothers" are earning income with the location being the point of differentiation. Finally, the "part-time working mother" is employed by someone else but works fewer than 40 hours a week. It's time to update the vernacular in which we refer to moms and their level of employment. We asked our Millennial Moms if they felt most of their peers aspired to be what would be known as the traditional "stay-at-home mom." The results showed that two to one, our moms answered, "No."

## #TakeNote

As a marketing professional, you may wonder why this tip is important to you. If you work with Mom Bloggers, it's important to recognize that most bloggers are in the business to make money. They consider themselves business owners and at-home working mothers. Remembering this fact will help you define business opportunities with bloggers that meet your respective goals and establish a mutually beneficial relationship. They want you as a brand to respect them as a business owner and they will reward you for it.

## #118 Finding yourself has become formalized — welcome to the gap year.

Searching for purpose is nothing new for a recent high school or college graduate, but younger Millennials have given it a name and made it chic: the gap year. It's a widely accepted year between high school and college, and sometimes between college and a career. It's so widely accepted now that college applications have a designated area where they ask applicants to note activities and experiences during a gap year. Organized gap-year programs offer adventures abroad, volunteer programs with a purpose and cultural learning experiences. It's big business and Baby Boomer parents are footing the bill to foster their Millennial children's desire to find themselves and their purpose in life. Life's too short for Millennials to invest in an education that leads them to a job they hate or a career that isn't fulfilling. A gap year allows them to make a conscious decision about their future. For companies who typically target consumers with graduation gift ideas, it is important to recognize this new trend. The typical assortment of engraved pens and gift cards may not meet the growing market of graduates who would rather have backpacks and hiking boots.

## #119 It's not her mother's feminism.

The Millennial Mom watched her mother strive for something that wasn't attainable, but she believes she has the tools and opportunity to achieve what her mother didn't. She is picking up where her mom left off. Instead of pursuing a balanced lifestyle, the Millennial Mom's goal is to create an integrated life for herself. The Millennial Mom, through choice and the use of technology, feels that she's in control of work-life issues. She knows she can have it all, but she chooses which parts of "all" she has at any given time. She's added new elements to the conversation about work-life and motherhood.

My prediction is that in light of this attitude, equal pay for women will become a bigger political issue by 2020. Thanks to Leanin.org, commercials with high-profile male and female celebrities are bringing the issue of fair pay for women to the forefront. As we are about to see, it won't be because the Millennial Mom is motivated by money. Her motivation will be fairness.

## #120 Millennial Moms seek out mentors.

Mentorship is the perfect combination of learning from others and respecting her elders. I remember a few years ago I received a sudden wave of emails from younger women asking if I would be willing to mentor them. When I say a wave, I am not exaggerating; it was no fewer than 10 a month. I couldn't figure out if these women wanted to steal my trade secrets for business and parenting or wiggle themselves into a job. Then I realized that overnight, a new generation of women was entering the workforce: Millennials. Millennials are eager to learn and they seek out experts to teach them.

Along with online search tools, mentors are rated as a top resource for Mom Inventors who have an idea and want to grow a business from it. Huggies MomInspired grant winners offer a glimpse of how mentors have provided invaluable advice and support.

## #TakeNote

Brands can connect with Millennial Moms by providing them with mentors. It's time to bring recipe testers who once had a place in a lab to the forefront of your brand.

*"I asked other women in business, and I have mentors who are far more successful than I am. So the company I keep helps me rise."*—Lisa Cash Hanson, CEO, Snuggwugg, Inc.

*"The Mompact group of mom inventors has been by far the best group I have been in for getting real help."*—Barbara Schantz, President and CEO, Baby Dipper, LLC

## #121 Millennial Moms are the first generation of women whose moms can be their personal and professional mentors.

Think about it. Boomer moms were the first generation of women who held numerous executive and professional titles in the workforce. In the last three decades they have risen to C-suites and built successful businesses as entrepreneurs. They are in the position of not only advising their daughters on family matters but business matters as well. The Millennial Mom has a resource that no other generation has had: her well-rounded, experienced and educated mother.

## #TakeNote

Don't be afraid to leverage the bond between mom and daughter. There is a lot of combined buying power with Boomer and Millennial mothers. In particular, I believe it's a great strategy for financial institutions that serve small businesses to showcase both generations in their marketing.

# #122 The Millennial Mom will give up income for flexibility and family time.

Flexibility is as important to a Millennial Mom as income when it comes to considering a new position or career. Her mom blazed the trail of work-life balance and fought for family benefits in the workplace and now she's here to collect them. You might say that she has known the importance of work flexibility since she was a baby. These were the first children to attend on-site daycare centers with moms who did job-sharing within corporate America. Now, as a mother herself, she feels entitled to reap the benefits of her mother's hard work.

# #123 Millennial Moms want work to be fun.

The Ping-Pong table is the symbol of the Millennial generation at work — and the new water cooler. Have you ever wondered why it's Ping-Pong? After all, it would be just as easy to have a pool table delivered to an office. Table tennis is a brain sport that involves fast thinking, movement, flexibility and quick decisions. These are all skills that Millennials take pride in possessing. Millennials want to have fun and enjoy time at the office, not only with Ping-Pong but also with beanbag chairs, board games and snacks in break rooms. In fact, the trend of Ping-Pong has grown so much as Millennials enter the workforce that a recent article asks, "Does the way a person approaches Ping-Pong correlate to the way they approach challenges in the workplace, and can the game be used as a predictive model?"[1] The results have not been released as of yet but I'm sure they will be interesting.

# #124 Make it engaging if you want to employ Millennial Moms.

Millennials now compose 34% of the workforce according to the Department of Labor Statistics, outnumbering Boomers and Gen Xers who represent 32% combined. By 2020, they will represent 46% of all U.S. workers.[2] They are a different force to be reckoned with in the office. Millennial Moms are proud of their skills and knowledge and are confident in applying them to work. They are free-thinking and motivated by projects. Their heavy use of Pinterest is a visible sign of their confidence in taking on new projects. They like to be challenged and find it difficult to understand strict rules and instructions around a task. They enjoy doing things their way and approach problem-solving in a carefree manner that can often be misunderstood by Boomers.

For employers, Millennials can be challenging. Retention is a problem because they get bored easily and if they don't feel challenged, they will move on. Grey Global Group took an interesting approach to engaging Millennials in the workplace. They placed all their Millennial associate executives in the same area. This created a vibe that resonated with these younger employees and increased productivity as well as creativity. Employers have a lot to gain from this innovative, risk-taking generation; they just need to take the time to understand their talents and behaviors.

## #125 The motivation to work from home is multidimensional.

One would hypothesize that moms who earn income at home work for the supplemental income. Surprisingly, more than 40% of Millennial Moms say that they engage in business activities at home to have an identity outside of their children. This might explain why moms who blog cringe at being referred to as a Mommy Blogger. If you look at the business cards of these women, you'll see titles such as Social Media Content Manager, Writer or Digital Content Provider — but rarely Mom Blogger. Another 37% work in order to use their abilities or pursue a passion. This is all-important for marketers to understand because it illustrates how important her own identity is to her self-image. She seeks to preserve her personal identity while enjoying her role as a mom. Brands who want to connect with the Millennial Mom need to be her partner in reaching this goal by speaking to her as a woman *and* a mother. Dove has done a great job at empowering the self-image of moms as women and has been rewarded for it with growing sales.

# #126 Mom Inventors aren't afraid of failure.

Millennials believe they can do anything and now is their chance to prove it. Millennial Moms are starting businesses every day. According to a 2014 BabyCenter.com survey of Millennial Moms, 39% of them are selling homemade items via social media. Over 35% have promoted their moneymaking endeavors on social media and at least 15% have received payment for running errands for others. They use technology to source product, file patents and build businesses. The most common time for a mom to invent a product is in the first two years after the birth of a child. This is the time when she discovers new challenges and with them, possible solutions.

Allyson Phillips invented the Tilty Cup when she watched her toddler struggle to drink from a real cup. Lisa Feder designed Zippyz while struggling to change her baby's diaper in the middle of the night. Neither of these women had a background in manufacturing. They used technology to find the means to source and launch their product idea. The second phase that tends to launch Mom Businesses is when their child goes to preschool or kindergarten. Suddenly, she has 4 – 6 hours of free time in her day and she will often launch a business. This has been the standard for many years but the younger Millennial crowd is bringing business into motherhood with them. Brands that recognize the business side of motherhood will uncover additional opportunities to connect with powerful influencers.

There are several brands that have reaped the rewards of connecting with Mom Business owners. The Huggies MomInspired program, a grant initiative created by BSM Media for Kimberly-Clark, was launched to help fund new product ideas invented by moms. It was not only a marketing program, but also a channel for Kimberly-Clark to identify new inventions that could potentially be licensed by the company. There was no shortage of applicants submitting existing products. My point is that historically, motherhood creates opportunities for moms to start businesses that don't deter them as one might expect. These Huggies MomInspired grant recipients reinforce the idea:

*"I was always talking about franchising, starting my own business and even doing an 'executive-like' cleaning service with chocolates on the pillows. I just needed something other than being at home raising babies . . . I sat at my desk and thought of what I needed (not my kids) to help me 'simplify life' with four girls. That's when I came up with the idea for a portable chair, with a sun bonnet, so that I could have the perfect 'parking spot' for my baby. That's when the Go With Me Chair was conceived. So I guess the ideas came from having kids and me having a need to manage my life with them better, especially when we went places."—Kristi Gorinas, Mompreneur, founder and CEO of the Kristi G Company*

*"I had a great idea for a diaper–changing helper and Snuggwugg was born. I wanted to build upon that and build a company that would create financial freedom for myself and others."—Lisa Cash Hanson, CEO, Snuggwugg, Inc.*

*"I started the Baby Dipper, LLC, because I thought there was a need for a product like mine that would enable parents to feed infants using only one hand."—Barbara Schantz, President and CEO, Baby Dipper, LLC*

# #127 Celebrity moms are becoming mompreneurs.

Jessica Alba and Rosie Pope became moms who later launched a business focused on mom consumers. An older set of celebrity moms have made their way into the Mom Business

### Celebrity Mompreneurs and Their Businesses

Jessica Alba - The Honest Company
Rosie Pope - Rosie Pope Maternity
Gwen Stefani - L.A.M.B.
Bethenny Frankel - Skinnygirl Cocktails
Jessica Simpson - The Jessica Simpson Collection
Nicole Richie - House of Harlow 1960
Kourtney & Kim Kardashian - DASH
Jennifer Lopez - J.Lo by Jennifer Lopez
Kate Hudson - Fabletics

as well but took a different approach. Felicity Huffman and Terri Hatcher both have websites for moms. Brooke Burke Charvet purchased Modernmom.com. Although these women speak online in a peer-to-peer voice, few Millennial Moms believe they are moms just like them.

## #128 Millennial Mompreneurs aren't afraid of sharks.

Grab the popcorn and gather around the television to watch ABC's *Shark Tank* and you are likely to see a Millennial Mom or two among the featured entrepreneurs. The show certainly is appealing for multiple generations. It illustrates the power of the American dream and so much more for Millennials. It offers an opportunity for Millennials to flex their creative muscles and demonstrate their innovative thinking. I've been excited to see so many mompreneurs featured on *Shark Tank*. These women serve as inspiration for Millennial mothers who have an idea and the will to pursue it. For marketers who want to hire spokespeople or partner with a mom who others look up to, I suggest mining the mom contestants on *Shark Tank*. There is not only an opportunity to attach your brand to their credibility in the marketplace, but a smart retailer would feature mom-made products. There is a huge untapped opportunity for brands to enter the Mom Market through the mom-made product door.

### Mompreneurs Who Have Appeared on Shark Tank

Kiersten Hathcock - Mod Mom Furniture
Dr. Amy Baxter - MMJ Labs, Makers of Buzzy®
Romy Taormina - Psi Health Solutions, Makers of Psi Bands
Bobbie Rhoads - Funbites®
Stephanie Parker - Sleeping Baby™, Makers of Zipadee-Zip
Rachel McMurtrey - Jungle Jumparoo
Tiffany Krumins - AVA the Elephant®

# #129 Millennials Moms are the first generation to call social media a business.

Thanks to the efforts of Gen Xer moms who started blogs and became accidental entrepreneurs, Millennial Moms can earn a living by building their own social media brand. Most Mom Bloggers today run businesses that go beyond payment for a product review. Today, these tech-savvy mothers earn income by training older users how to utilize social media, managing social channels for smaller local businesses or producing digital content for other brands. It's a legitimate job with a respectable income that provides flexibility, an outlet for creativity and the opportunity to stay connected with others.

*The impact of the*
*Great Recession in*
*late 2007 taught*
*Millennial Moms*
*that the economy*
*can deliver unexpected*
*situations; therefore*
*controlling her financial*
*future is important.*

# CHAPTER
# 6

## Finances

# #130 Wealthy Millennials are few in numbers.

Only 1% of Millennials make $106,000 a year or more according to the Census Bureau's Current Population Survey. That's almost one million of the 83 million, and they control about double the income of the 15 million Millennials in the bottom 18% of the population. The 1% includes 7% Hispanic and 30% female. An astonishing statistic is that 28 million out of the 83 million aren't in school and earn less than $10,000 a year, according to the last census numbers. The top profession among Millennials is lawyers followed by managers, according to Census Bureau data.

# #131 Millennial Moms enter adulthood with debt.

Millennial Moms are as likely to have a mortgage and credit card debts as they are to have college loan debts. According to our survey, 44% of Millennial Moms said they had the burden of education loans at graduation compared to 31% of Gen X mothers. Paying off these loans is constantly on their minds while 70% of Millennial Moms said they worry about their personal debt.

Millennials share a record $1.2 trillion in student loan debt, compounded by an unemployment rate among 18-to-29-year-olds of 15%.[1] College debt, a soft job market and the ready availability of technology to help them save money has made many of these women more frugal in nature.

# #132 "Alpha earner" is the new prenup for Millennial couples.

Ring. Bouquet. Work plan. It's all a part of the planning for Millennial couples. Who is going to stay home with the kids is often decided before they walk down the aisle. Forty percent of Millennial Moms discussed with their intended spouses who will be the alpha earner once their children were born. This is reflective of Millennial Moms being comfortable in the role of breadwinner *or* primary caregiver.

# #133 Millennial Moms seek financial security.

The impact of the Great Recession in late 2007 taught them that the economy can deliver unexpected situations; therefore controlling her financial future is important. Many Millennial Moms impose saving restrictions on their spending in order to establish a process toward obtaining financial security. The creative side of Millennial Moms starts to show as they figure out ways to pick up a few dollars anywhere they can. There are still many marketing professionals who don't fully understand how Mom Bloggers make money through their social channels. These innovative women join affiliate programs that pay commissions on everything from selling coupons online to building databases on behalf of brands. This is in addition to the banner campaigns they run on their blogs and of course paid reviews and brand partnerships. Later I'll talk about the Millennial Mom and her shopping behaviors, but for now, keep in mind that most of these women will not purchase a product online without first searching for a discount code. They like to save, whether it's on their purchases or through dollars in the bank. Fortunately for them, there are plenty of blogs out there that focus on savings, coupons and discounts or teach them how to pinch pennies.

# #134 Millennials plan for their financial future.

I've discussed the impact that the slowed economy of 2007 had on the Millennial. They learned at an early age how the instability of the markets and loss of jobs could impact families. For this reason, financial planning is important to them. You often hear younger Millennials justify living at home after college as a way to save money. Perhaps this is as true as is the inability to find work, which many have contributed to this trend. There are estimates stating that close to 25% of college graduates with jobs are living at home.[2]

Millennials want to feel secure financially before they leave the nest and living at home for a few years allows them to do this. It's interesting to note, however, that life insurance policies are at historic lows among Millennials. According to a Life Insurance Management and Research Association (LIMRA) report, only 34% of Millennials own an individual policy, and only 20% plan on purchasing a policy. I would argue that this declining interest in life insurance begins to change once the Millennials have children. At the time of LIMRA's research, less than one-third of all Millennials had children. Additionally, I would suggest that Millennials plan for everyday financial stability, rather than for the long-term; they saw how that was lost when their parent lost his/her job in 2008. They are thinking more about keeping the lights on if their job is cut rather than the loss of income in the event of an untimely demise. Don't forget the Millennial seeks instant gratification. Seeing a hundred bucks in the bank is far more fulfilling than paying toward a policy for the unforeseeable future. The concept doesn't strike the right chords for a Millennial.

# #135 They seek financial advice from their parents.

Younger Millennials in particular go to their mothers and fathers for money advice. It's important to note that I'm not saying they go to their parents for a loan. They are looking for the "should I" or "shouldn't I" answers. Part of this behavior can be attributed to their age and stage of life, but more likely it's the outcome of their childhood. The insecurities of the economy and watching their parents live through it have instilled a cautious attitude along with respect for their parents' financial wisdom.

## #TakeNote

It's likely that both older and younger Millennials will use the same investment firms as their parents. For banks and other financial institutions, this becomes a marketing opportunity. Images of multigenerational clients connect with both the Millennial and her Boomer parents. AIG did a good job with a series of ads they ran in late 2014. They portrayed a

Millennial being able to pick up the tab while having dinner with his father. It worked because it empowered the Millennial, yet demonstrated that AIG was a brand the older generation trusted. Financial security is very important to the Millennial. The more a brand can offer assistance in helping her reach this goal, the more likely she is to build up loyalty to that brand.

# #136  Finances are a team sport.

While not all tasks are evenly split in Millennial households, the majority of Millennial Moms (53%) in our survey say that they and their partner are equally responsible for financial decisions. Communication is key, with 37% discussing all purchases with their significant others. It's common for couples in all generations to have a spending threshold at which they discuss purchases and this rings true for Millennials as well. For 46% of Millennials, that threshold is somewhere between $50 and $200.

*Millennial Moms*

*place a premium*

*on products or*

*services that*

*save them time.*

# CHAPTER
# 7

## Shopping

# #137 The Great Recession made an impact on Millennials' shopping behaviors.

The National Bureau of Economic Research dates the Great Recession from approximately late 2007 through 2010, although many would argue the economy is still sluggish and only showed marked improvement in 2014. For the Millennial, the timing could not have been worse. Many of the oldest Millennials were entering the workforce in 2007 when unemployment and student loan payments were high. I've already discussed how launching into adulthood in the middle of a recession has impacted their political views, but the greatest impact is found in their spending behaviors.

# #138 Millennial Moms have their own shopping style.

We asked Millennial Moms to compare their shopping styles to their moms' behaviors. According to the results, Millennials are more likely to be frugal and less likely to make impulse purchases.

### Shopping Style of Millennial Moms VS Their Mothers

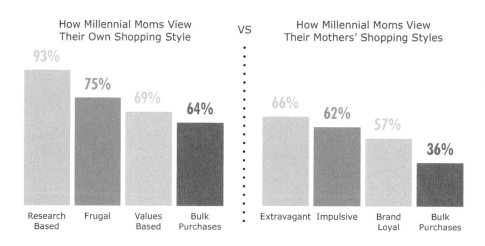

# #139 The Millennial Mom doesn't like to shop alone and her mom is a top companion of choice.

Gone are the days when shopping with Mom was embarrassing (insert eye roll). Millennials grew up shopping with their mothers and have fond memories of trips to the mall for shopping sprees. Visits to H&M, Forever 21 and Macy's usually resulted in a purchase for her by her indulgent mom. It was a good time. As an adult, she likes to have company when she shops. Often it's a spouse or significant other, which is easy since Millennial Dads shop more than any other generation of fathers in history. However, the more popular choice for a store-browsing companion is her own mother.

A majority of Millennial Moms (77%) say they went shopping with their mother at least once a week while growing up. In some ways, the mothers of Millennials (now grandmothers) are still blazing a trail to the cash register. This is an opportunity for those brands that are smart enough to market to grandparents as a way of attracting Millennial Moms to their products.

If the Millennial Mom heads off to the mall alone, her friends are only a text, post or Snapchat away. An overwhelming 81% of Millennial Moms say they use their cell phone to ask someone outside of the store for input on a buying decision.

# #140 She's frugal but she isn't cheap.

Spending tradeoffs exist for the Millennial Moms. Everyday items like consumable products, personal clothing and general household items are areas where moms say they are more likely to save money. Certain big-ticket items like cars also fall in the "save" category for almost 82% of moms in the survey. Splurge areas for her are in the category of health and beauty products and electronics. Other areas where she will spend a little more include special occasions and celebrations (67%), travel and vacation (56%) and dining out and gifts (54%).

# #141 She splurges on experiences and celebrations for her family, while saving on more practical items.

While she might enter the grocery store with a virtual "stack" of coupons (72% save on groceries), Millennial Moms aren't afraid to splurge where it counts. Because they're all about celebrating to the fullest and elevating everyday moments to special occasions, it's no surprise that 65% of Millennial Moms reported splurging on celebrations for her family. Those perfectly coordinated Pinterest parties don't come cheap and she's willing to pay extra for the details that will make her photos Instagram-worthy.

Experiences are also worth the investment in their eyes; 55% splurge on them for their families. The same mom who stockpiles dish soap might be more than happy to shell out money for gymnastics classes, zoo passes or tickets to *Disney On Ice*.

# #142 Her children are dressed in the latest fashions, while playing with hand-me-down toys.

It comes as no surprise that fashion-conscious Millennials view their children as extensions of their personal style. Outfitting Millennial offspring has become an indulgence for moms, with 57% saying that they splurge on clothes for their children. Many turn their noses up at mass-produced, gender-specific onesies (Mommy's New Man, Daddy's Team Captain), preferring instead more unique apparel that more closely resembles shrunken versions of their own wardrobe, from distressed jeans to "vintage" concert t-shirts. Surprisingly, only 18% of moms said that they splurge on clothes for themselves. It could be that they've cracked the code to dressing well on a budget, or can more easily resist adding to their own wardrobes.

If clothes are a splurge, toys are a save, with 72% of Millennial Moms describing themselves as frugal in that area. That doesn't mean the playrooms of Millennial kids are bare. Moms are just seeking out cost-effective methods for amassing new playthings. From swapping with friends to repurposing household items, Millennial Moms aren't afraid to get creative to manage both cost and space considerations. Subscription-based toy boxes, such as Sparkbox Toys (dubbed the Netflix of toys), allow moms to regularly refresh their little one's toy chest by renting and returning toys specific to their child's age.

# #143 Millennial Moms are willing to pay to save time.

Millennial Moms place a premium on products or services that save them time. So much so that a whopping 83% of these moms are often willing to pay more for a product or service that offers a return of valuable time. Specific areas rate high for the tradeoff of money for time. Starting with the most popular, Millennial Moms will shell out more money for products in these categories:

### Millennial Moms Will Pay More for These Products to Save Time

58% Meal Planning/Food Prep

51% Household Chores

46% Technology

38% Travel

36% Beauty Products

28% Health & Wellness

19% Fitness

When these moms do not want to pay a higher price and ultimately forgo the time-saving payoff, more than half (53%) say their motivations are quality, followed by a sense of accomplishment (45%), enjoyment of the task or activity (44%) and the all-important customization (35%) that all Millennial Moms expect from products and services. They're willing to spend more to save time, but not at the expense of quality. So even though it might be quicker and cheaper for a Millennial Mom to bake brownies using a boxed mix, it's just as likely she'll opt for the from-scratch version.

# #144 Millennial Moms define value as a combination of price and quality.

Value is a topic that remains constant among generations although it ranks higher in the decision-making process for Millennial Mothers. For this reason, I want to spend some time discussing how moms define value. First, let's first talk about what it's not. "Value" does not mean "cheap." A mom seeking value is *not* looking for the cheapest product. Again, value is a combination of price and quality. I called it Mom Math in my book *Trillion Dollar Moms*: quality + performance + benefits = value.

Millennial Moms, like their parents, will trade up and down. They will carry a $200 Michael Kors purse but shop for their bathing suit at Target. The Millennial Mom will establish the parameters of the tradeoff by doing extensive research online and among her family and friends. The investment of this time is valuable in finding a quality product the first time around. She doesn't have the time to reinvest in buying a replacement product. She's willing to pay a little more if she knows that she is gaining quality from the product.

Benefits come into play as well for the Millennial Mom. These might include loyalty reward earnings like free product or future discounts, access to exclusive product and the ability to customize delivery of a service.

## #TakeNote

Marketers should take a step back and look at the overall value of the product. Speak to the real-life application of the product to the mom's family. For instance, it's one thing to position a $10 pizza as a great deal. However, if it's a healthy meal option that everyone in the family will enjoy, that's a much stronger message. Dealing in discounts only isn't the best approach to Millennials. They like to feel wise about their purchases, so give them a reason to feel like they made the right choice in buying your product. Just being another $10 coupon-lover might work today, but it won't keep the Millennial Mom coming back.

*"Value is quality at a good price. For instance, I'd buy consignment clothes and get long-lasting brands rather than shop at Walmart where the clothes give out. Likewise for food, I can't afford organic (and hey — we are all going to die someday) but I buy real food at good prices by shopping sales. We don't buy Oreos or packaged cookies — we make our own bread (bc it's good quality and pennies per loaf)."—Sierra R., 35*

*"A quality item that is helpful for the amount I have to pay or time to use it."—Lark H., 31*

## #145 Millennial Moms are coupon lovers.

All moms like to save money by using coupons. What sets Millennial Moms apart, as with most distinguishing behaviors, is the use of technology (specifically their smartphones) to access coupons and money-saving apps. The "old-fashioned" paper coupons are still popular with Millennial Moms with almost 70% using them at some point. However, discount codes edge out paper coupons with 75% of these same moms accessing them from their phones to get their deals. Slightly more than half (53%) use mobile "saving" apps in lieu of paper coupons, and I expect this number to keep increasing.

When asked about coupon use, over 54% of moms surveyed said they frequently use coupons, versus an average of 21% of moms who "always" use coupons and 20% who "sometimes" use them. Coupon use definitely evokes an emotional feeling for all moms, and Millennials are no different. The majority of Millennial Moms report feeling practical (59%), happy (58%), satisfied (53%) and smart (49%) when they use coupons to save money.

## #TakeNote

Discount codes are the way to go with moms, particularly those shopping online. They are easy for moms to share on social media and allow brands to track usage. Make sure that you don't hold them hostage, requiring too much information before moms can access them. Remember, instant gratification is your friend when it comes to Millennial Moms.

# #146 Millennial Moms learn to save money through deal and coupon blogs.

There is a large community of deal, coupon and shopping blogs and Millennial Moms are taking advantage of their extensive shopping-savvy info. Marketers often minimize the level of influence these bloggers have online; however, they have millions of readers. Additionally, they have loyal followers who plan their weekly shopping activities with the help of these sites. The women who write these blogs take great pride in educating other women on how to save money.

Many marketers try to avoid working with coupon bloggers because they feel that the association with these blogs cheapens their product or brand. That may have been the case in the early 2000s when moms surfed the Internet for freebies. Today, the women who read frugal blogs are savvy shoppers who make very calculated buying decisions. Additionally, these blogs attract more mainstream moms who do not frequent parenting, travel and other lifestyle blogs.

## #TakeNote

I recommend giving deal and coupon bloggers another chance, particularly if you are a consumable product company or a brand that uses a lot of discounts to drive sales. One of my favorite tactics to use with frugal and coupon bloggers is to give them early notification of high-value coupons in the Sunday newspaper inserts. Giving moms the exclusive first access to this type of information will elevate them among their peers and they'll be more likely to share it with their followers, as it validates their expertise in this space.

# #147 Millennial Moms buy in-store only after doing online research.

Long before she enters a brick-and-mortar retailer, she is likely to have researched prices and features online. Fifty-five percent of moms say they sometimes buy a product offline after conducting online research, many times on a manufacturer or e-commerce site. Another 32% of Millennial Moms say they do this frequently. This is important to both traditional and online retailers.

There are times, however, when she does both: research and shop online. According to our research, Millennial Moms are most likely to purchase gifts, electronics and travel online. She does her online shopping between 8 pm and 10 pm. Close to 80% of moms know exactly what they want when they go online because they've already done their research. A mom in this category intentionally goes to the website where she will ultimately spend her money. Almost 63% of moms will choose a random website based on free shipping and 37% of moms say that a discount offered on Facebook will put a brand into consideration.

### #TakeNote

It is imperative for companies to ensure that moms can easily find the information they need to make their buying decisions. For the brick-and-mortar store, your online presence is as important as your point of purchase. The online retailer needs to work harder by offering benefits, such as free shipping and exclusive designs. You will likely find it beneficial to conduct a social audit to ensure that your information is distributed in multiple places. Check your mix of online content and make sure that moms can find reviews on YouTube, Pinterest and various blogs. If the content is there, make sure there's a fast and easy path to checkout.

## #148 Millennials desire the good life at a dollar-store price.

Many may have enjoyed Coach bags, manicures and $10 lattes growing up but they also saw the emergence of dollar stores. I know that the concept of inexpensive retailers is not new. I'm old enough to remember going to a Woolworth store with my grandmother. However, the expansion and emergence of retailers who exclusively offer $1 merchandise presented a new way of shopping to the Millennial generation.

There is a kind of cultural infatuation for seeing what one can create from merchandise purchased at a dollar store. Just visit Heather Mann's blog, www.dollarstorecrafts.com. She has over 250,000 fans on Facebook, 30,000 Vine followers and her blog has so much traffic that she has attracted major brands as sponsors and advertisers. Heather isn't alone in this space. Millennial Moms have created thousands of Pinterest boards dedicated to dollar-store creations. Everything from home decor to wedding receptions can come from the aisles of these discount retailers. Target took note of this trend and added $1 item displays at the front of their stores. My guess is that they're doing well with them, but I do think they could be doing better in sales presentation.

In my opinion, Target has made one mistake in their execution of selling $1 merchandise. Right in the middle of the dollar section, Target guests find $2 and sometimes $3 items. Insertion of higher-priced products takes the Millennial Mom out of her quest-for-creativity mode and puts her on guard such that she has to pay attention to the shopping experience. Target loses the mom who was immersed in her Pinterest dreams and willing to bring her ideas alive with their merchandise. They would be better served to use that shelf space for more $1 items and would most likely see greater turnover of that inventory. Marketers can successfully use the dollar strategy, but should not do it if it sends mixed messages to the Millennial Mom.

## #TakeNote

There are other ways to take advantage of this opportunity. Instead of marketing all your merchandise down to $1, I suggest focusing on the Millennial Mom's desire for frugal creativeness. Look at your product and also go to Pinterest. See what moms are doing with it in their creative moments. Either partner with Millennial Moms to share their creative ideas on your social media outlets or offer them some of your brand's creative ideas. Remember when I was talking about

Facebook and how many Millennial Moms enjoy thought-starters? These can be used to talk about your product aside from the way it was intended.

Before you let your agency or creative team loose on creating a thought-starter, I want to offer a bit of advice. Make sure that the idea will resonate with the greatest number of moms. Recently, Hefty released a four-part video series for their iconic red cups. Their target audience was Millennial Moms. They could have gone in several directions with their message but they chose to focus on what they called #PartyHardMoms. The videos featured older Millennial Moms talking in teen lingo about their after-hours social time while folding laundry and other mom tasks. There's a lot of debate as to whether these ads hit the target audience, and based on the comments I'm seeing on my Facebook page, it may not be resolved anytime soon.

My point in this example is that Hefty would have been better served to show moms sharing about all different uses for Hefty's red cups. On Pinterest I've seen them converted into everything from Minnie Mouse party decorations to wind chimes. I'm confident that focusing on this angle would have produced thousands, if not millions, of pages of consumer-generated content. It would leverage a behavior Millennial Moms are already doing: sharing dollar-store creations. Instead, Hefty produced expensive videos that a mom will watch once and maybe share if she relates to being a #PartyHardMom and move on. No shelf life, no spot on Pinterest and only one fleeting opportunity to post on their Facebook page. So take a look at your product through a different lens and you may uncover the sweet spot for Millennial Moms.

# #149 Smartphones are their shopping buddies.

While shopping, 61% of mothers use their smartphones to make lists, review suggestions, retrieve coupons and comparison shop.

**Top Comparison Shopping Sites/Apps Used by Moms**

| | |
|---|---|
| Amazon | Price Grabber |
| Bizrate | RedLaser |
| BuyVia | ShopSavvy |
| GasGuru | Shopzilla |
| Google Shopping | Smoopa |
| Kayak | TheFind |
| Nextag | TripAdvisor |

# #150 Millennial Moms are armed with electronic coupons.

The Millennial Mom's toolbox of savings is a mix of deals via emails, text coupons and apps. The use of electronic coupons is popular for this deal-seeking mom. The majority of Millennials (61%) have adopted the use of mobile savings apps into their shopping routines, compared to just 45% of Gen Xers. Savings don't just come via apps on their smartphones; 41% of Millennial Moms prefer to receive text coupons from brands and retailers. Mention mobile coupons and a Millennial Mom is likely to cite Jo-Ann's, Michaels Craft or Bed, Bath and Beyond as sources for discounts through text messages.

According to the Leo Burnett agency, there are four key elements of mobile marketing: deals, connecting with friends and family, saving time and entertainment. An effective tactic should have at least two of them. Starbucks' mobile app resonates with Millennial Moms because it offers timesaving payment options, rewards and entertainment in the form of free music downloads. Not surprisingly, 14% of their revenue comes from mobile transactions.[1]

In light of emerging technologies, marketers often forget about the effectiveness of emails when it comes to moms. Millennial Moms are tech-savvy and welcome emails that are relevant and timely. The Millennial Mom finds it relaxing to browse through images of your latest designs and loves arming herself with a good coupon when she goes shopping. If email is your delivery method of choice, remember that Millennial Moms, unlike previous generations of mothers, read email in the morning. To be at the top of the mom's unopened emails, send promotional emails in the morning before 7 am so that she can read them before the kids wake up.

My own experience in retail locations led me to ask Millennials about their mobile coupon consumption. I asked moms how often they searched for an electronic coupon on their wireless devices before they reached the cash register. The responses confirmed my theory that the search for electronic coupons is as much a part of the shopping behaviors of Millennials as is checking the past-due date on food items.

*"Every single time. I tend to do it at Best Buy and Old Navy the most (have no idea why). I am motivated by my need to get the best deal I can. My procrastination and forgetfulness make it hard to do the research beforehand. I use RetailMeNot a lot."*—Shari V.H., 33

*"Every single time. Michaels mostly. I don't even look at paper coupons anymore because I know I can find mobile ones."*—Heather K., 34

*"Every Single Time. I like to save money and I am probably the one in line who motivates the people behind me. I usually use the website."*—Sarah C., 32

*"I Google before getting in line, if I do not have the store app."*—Sommer P., 30

## #151 Millennial Moms have changed the rules of commerce.

Shopping has changed in so many ways, thanks to the Millennial Mom. Yes, the Generation X moms fueled the growth of online shopping but her younger cohort has added another dimension to shopping. Technology has no doubt been the tool that Millennial Moms have used to make shopping easier and more convenient. It has also allowed her to make smarter purchases. Close to 80% of Millennial Moms say they research an item online before purchasing it online or offline. Amazon taught them at a young age that product reviews and immediate delivery are available at their fingertips.

Think about it. Since she was a toddler, Amazon has been suggesting products, offering peer reviews and overnighting packages to her home. Brown boxes on the front porch are a common occurrence for a Millennial and her Post Generation children. Receiving a brown box in the mail for most Boomers meant that a grandparent was sending a birthday gift or it was the holiday season. Millennials don't think twice about signing for a FedEx package and most can tell you the name of their UPS driver.

Thanks to apps and websites like Red Laser and PriceGrabber, she can easily compare the price of an item at multiple retailers and save herself a lot of driving or surfing online. She can use product reviews to hone in on the right product for her family and attend auctions in private Facebook groups. Some of these practices might not be as well known among marketers as others. Let's look at a few of the ones I attribute to the Millennial Mom cohort.

Consensus shopping, also known as social shopping, was born with the camera phone. It's the practice of taking a photo at a store and posting it to Facebook or Instagram with the caption "A or B?" or "What do you think?" After all those years of a parent telling her children to be careful posting pictures on social media, we now have an entire generation of women who post pictures from the fitting room. As many as 90% of all Millennial Moms say they send photos to someone outside the store for their opinion. My advice to retailers: make sure you have great Wi-Fi in your stores if you want moms to share your merchandise with others.

 Reliable in-store WiFi is a must for brands that want #MillennialMoms to share product photos while shopping.

Another form of social shopping can be found on Facebook. It happens on personal pages and in private groups. Here's how it works. Let's say I have a gently used crib, so I post about it as my status to sell or trade it with a follower who needs the item. This is simple bartering that has been going on for decades;

however, this time the trade can happen within seconds and in the palm of my hand and not in classified ads. No more driving to the consignment store. Some innovative moms integrated the concept into their mom-focused Facebook groups, where members regularly hold auctions for baby items. These Millennial Moms use technology to stretch their dollar while gaining the fulfillment of helping out a friend who needs something another person no longer wants.

Loyalty marketing has long been an element of shopping but Millennial Moms have added their own twist here as well. The frugal and money-smart shoppers have taken reward shopping to another level. They are using apps such as Whengage.com and Shopkick.com to earn cash and rewards by visiting retailers, restaurants and service providers. Whengage.com allows moms to collect a cash reward for visiting companies and sampling their products. It's great for a mom who might be in that area with a few minutes to spare before school pickup.

Finally, a discussion about shopping behaviors wouldn't be complete without talking about the impact of apps. I'll be providing several dedicated Facts about apps. For now, I think we can all agree that apps have allowed the Millennial Mom to take her Internet research into the retail environment. It's not uncommon for a mom to search for a better price or a coupon on her smartphone before placing a product into her cart. She can find recipes for in-store sale items and coordinate the purchase of products from multiple stores while in line to check out.

## #TakeNote

The Millennial Mom is an empowered shopper, and my best advice to brands is to get in step with her. Provide her with the tools she wants and needs to make good buying decisions. Empower her with the knowledge you have about your product, not only from a features and benefits perspective but also with practical applications as well. This may mean you have to enlist the help of her peers to provide your brand with reviews, how-to videos, end-product images and craft ideas. It's all the things she has on her mind for your product but that may not be on yours.

**and Checklist for the Millennial Mom Shopper**

- ✓ Product Reviews on Website & Social Media
- ✓ "How To" Videos on YouTube & MomTV
- ✓ Product Reviews on Blogs
- ✓ Video Product Reviews on Amazon
- ✓ Mobile Coupons
- ✓ Discounts & Sneak Peeks on Social Media
- ✓ Product Ideas on Pinterest

## #152 Millennials are open to online payment solutions, rather than using credit cards.

Only 63% of Millennials said they had used a credit card in the past year, according to a recent consumer insights report.[2] Instead, they are adopters of Starbucks' mobile payment option, Apple Pay, online pizza ordering, etc., and are open to using bitcoin.

While #MillennialMoms may find ways to save in the grocery store, they are willing to splurge on celebrations and experiences.

## #153 Transparency in reviews is a must with Millennial Moms.

It's worth mentioning this again. There are few traits more critical to moms than transparency. Just as with any relationship, trust is imperative. Moms want to be able to trust that the review she's reading on your website is credible. She wants to know that she can trust the information she sees on your Facebook page and Twitter feed. Millennial Moms are smart and they are connected, as we know. They will expose brands that stretch the truth and defy her trust. It's never a good decision to pay people to write positive reviews on sites like Yelp, TripAdvisor or Amazon.

# #154 Loyalty programs are important to Millennial Moms.

Over three-fourths, or 77%, of Millennial Moms participate in retailer loyalty programs, according to research done by Harris Interactive on behalf of the Canadian loyalty company Aimia. In addition, there are hundreds of Mom Blogs devoted to maximizing the benefits of loyalty programs at retailers like CVS and Walgreens.

Millennial Moms expect programs to be free, easy and fast. They enjoy being rewarded. They almost expect to obtain something for just showing up in your store, much like it was in their childhood when they received a trophy for participation. However, they want the rewards to be obtainable through purchases that are relevant to their everyday lives, with redemption policies and steps that are easy and clearly defined.

Loyalty can be measured and leveraged with products as well as retailers. Gerber recently leveraged this Millennial characteristic in a campaign for their Win-Win program. After purchasing 10 Gerber Graduates products, consumers could upload the receipt to receive a Gerber gift set. The program was well received because it had clear deliverables for the Millennial Mom, easy-to-follow directions and an exclusive reward at the end.

# #155 Cause marketing is effective in connecting with Millennial Moms.

When asked what means the most when purchasing products and services, Millennial Moms ranked traditional factors at the top (price, quality, convenience), as expected. However, the values of the brand ranked higher than the brand name, product longevity and style or appearance of the product.

According to a Punchbowl trend blog, 54% of Millennial women indicated that they switched brands because it supported a cause they cared about.

As a socially responsible generation, Millennials have driven the explosion of cause marketing. Cause sponsorship spending reached $1.85 billion in 2014, an increase of 3.9% over 2013, and 2015 is expected to increase another 3.7% to $1.92 billion this year.[3] Toms Shoes, Box Tops for Education and Ben & Jerry's

(Scoop It Forward) are just a few of the brands that have aligned with social good.

## #TakeNote

It's important to remember when engaging in cause marketing that Millennials want your efforts to be authentic. They can spot a marketing campaign from a mile away. Your cause marketing programs should make sense for your brand and demonstrate a long-term commitment. Giving back, social good and community service — these initiatives are all well received by the Millennial Mom who believes she can make a difference and wants the brands she purchases to do so as well.

*"Toms for instance gives back to the less fortunate. It makes me feel good that when I purchase an item they give an item to someone who wouldn't normally be able to get it."—Amy, 30*

*"I buy from companies like Warby Parker who gives a pair of glasses to a needy person for every pair that I purchase. I like to know they are giving back to others."—Jennifer B., 35*

*"I love buying the Kohl's Cares line. I get great books for my kids all while the net profits help kids all over. I like when my purchase can make a difference."—Dawn N., 34*

## #156 She seeks authenticity and buys local.

Millennials seek out authenticity in many parts of their lives, including their purchases. They are making concerted efforts to shop locally and buy from independent retailers instead of big box stores. Shopping locally and supporting indie retailers makes Millennials feel good about their purchases, their communities and their impact on the environment.[4] They like knowing where their products are coming from and that the sellers are passionate people who care about the quality of their work. This desire for authenticity in their purchases is one of the things that fuel the growth of sites like Etsy.

Millennials are turning to Etsy to buy everything from handmade clothes and jewelry to vintage furnishings and letterpress stationery. Through online marketplaces like these, Millennials are able to seek out exactly what they're looking for, instead of having their purchases and product availability dictated by national sales campaigns. The search for local, authentic flavors has fueled many industries, from craft beers and fair-trade coffees to farmers' markets.

*The generation that*

*spent their childhood*

*with parents who*

*marked milestones with*

*celebrations and praise*

*has discovered ways*

*to keep themselves in*

*the spotlight.*

# CHAPTER
# 8

## Millennial Made

# #157 Millennial Moms are creators of new holidays.

Hallmark may have created holidays like Boss's Day but Millennials can take credit for gender-reveal parties and half-birthdays, among others. The generation that spent their childhood with parents who marked milestones with celebrations and praise has discovered ways to keep themselves in the spotlight. The Millennial generation has created reasons to gather: as expectant couples to reveal the gender of their unborn child or to travel on a "babymoon" prior to delivery.

The following facts speak to the new holidays, celebrations and milestones that Millennials have created as a generation:

• 30% of Millennials create and send "expecting" announcements as a formal way to share their pregnancy news.

• 15% of these new mothers have enjoyed babymoons and received push presents. (In case you're not familiar with the term, a "push present" is a gift a mom receives after delivery in appreciation for giving birth, hence the "push" part.)

• Almost 20% plan gender-reveal events, big and small, as well as monthly events celebrating baby's first year.

## #TakeNote

These new traditions provide smart marketers with the opportunity to be part of the celebrations and open new channels for sales. Likewise, babymoons present travel services and destination resorts a whole new market of consumers with slightly different needs and goals than that of the honeymoon market or the family clientele. Tapping into the babymoon market might lead a travel destination to offer foot massages, elongated pillows for comfortable pregnancy sleeping and nonalcoholic specialty drinks. It's important to understand this Millennial phenomenon in order to identify opportunities for your business or product.

# #158 **Gender-reveal parties are a Millennial Mom thing.**

Somewhere between the plus sign on a stick and labor/delivery is another hallmark of pregnancy for many couples: finding out if baby-to-be is a he or a she. Unlike past generations, many Millennial Moms aren't content with simply watching an ultrasound technician point out anatomy on a screen. No, they want to customize this moment as well as bringing their friends and family into the celebration. What started out as a fun act of cutting a cake to reveal pink or blue icing has turned into a full-blown party occasion, complete with gender-betting pools and party favors. Pinterest and Instagram have no doubt contributed to this trend, with a seemingly endless array of ideas for revealing baby's gender, from balloons hidden in a box to piñatas filled with confetti and candy. Sometimes the parents-to-be are in on the reveal while other times they are surprised right alongside their guests. The verdict and reactions are quickly shared over social media to announce the news. Gender-reveal parties are just another way Millennial Moms are embracing this new stage in their lives and taking every opportunity to celebrate.

Having a pulse on how Millennials are using product to incorporate into events like gender-reveal parties can create incremental sales. Here's an example I discovered on Facebook a few years ago and brought to the attention of Build-A-Bear Workshop. Expectant couples were going into Build-A-Bear stores with their sonogram photos and asking associates to build a bear as represented in the sonogram. Now before you wonder how the associate could read a sonogram, don't fret. The Millennial would ask the doctor to write the gender on the back of the photo and seal it in an envelope. They would then give the sealed envelope to the BABW associate and ask them to build a bear representative of the gender indicated on the back of the sonogram. The pink or blue bear would be placed in the well-known Bear Cub Condo and there it would stay, unidentified to even the expectant parents. After assembling family and friends for a party, the couple opens the box and discovers the gender of their baby surrounded by friends and family. A pink bear of course means a girl and a blue bear a boy. The opportunity for Build-A-Bear was to create a special baby bear, birth certificate and bear accessories. I'm sure you're getting my point: Build-A-Bear has taken advantage of this opportunity to capture a whole new market of consumers.

*"After finding out the gender of my second child at the doctor's office, I knew exactly who I needed to call first. Nope, not my mom or BFF. I called the event planners at my local Panera Bread who had offered to help me reveal the gender of my little one to my friends and family. Within just a few hours, I arrived at my local Panera Bread and adorable boxes of cookies were waiting for me, enclosed in white boxes that said 'He or She . . . Open to See.' I gathered my parents, in-laws and grandparents (with my brother tuning in via FaceTime) for the big reveal. They ripped open the boxes to find cookies with PINK M&M's — we were having a girl! I also sent some cookies into preschool with my son so he could share the sweet surprise of getting a baby sister with his friends. After the gender reveal, I shared the details on my blog so that my friends and followers would think of Panera for their next special occasion. It was a day I will never forget and can't wait to share the pictures with my daughter one day."—Amy G., 32*

*"We did a gender reveal to announce our daughter. We had a get-together with close family and friends at a local clubhouse. To announce the gender, we wrapped a sign that we had created that said 'It's a Girl!' in layers of blue and pink paper. We had the great-grandparents sit together and pass the package around, each one unwrapping a layer until they got to the end. We researched different blogs and Pinterest for ideas. Combining a few different ideas, I came up with the idea to pass around the wrapped package. We had a gender reveal because we wanted a fun way to announce our daughter's gender. Plus, she was the first grandchild for both my in-laws and parents, so we wanted to make it fun for them."— Krystal C., 30*

*"I enjoy seeing the creative ways friends share, and my family is spread out all over so we've done announcements since we don't always see them. Some I only see once a year. I know when I was little my mom also sent out cards with photos often. Nowadays we*

*rarely print anything. Announcements & holiday cards are the only time I print anything out. Bump photos is also something new. I did them religiously with my first pregnancy. And less regularly with my second."—Melissa D., 33*

## # 159 Friendly competition exists among Millennial Moms.

It starts with the gender reveal, followed by the birth announcement, and it grows with the planning of her child's first birthday party. It's called friendly competition. Moms love to outdo other moms, even if it's lighthearted competition. Don't believe me? Check out Pinterest and, while you're there, search #PinterestFail and see how many Millennial Moms are attempting to do extraordinary things with recycled crafts, birthday favors and holiday tables. The good news for marketers is that it's a behavior that can be leveraged to drive sales and increase product consumption. Rice Krispies is a great example of finding growth in friendly competition. The "average" mom makes the traditional square Rice Krispies treats, but the "overachieving mom" makes Halloween-shaped characters for the class party. Seeing an opportunity to leverage friendly competition among mothers, Rice Krispies now regularly posts recipes for seasonal-themed treats on their boxes and social media.

### #TakeNote

To discover how moms are using your product to show off their talents among their peers, check out Pinterest. You're likely to be amazed by the ways Millennial Moms are applying their creativity to your product.

## # 160 Millennial Moms arrive into motherhood with a push present.

Along with a bouncing new addition and a birth story she can use to terrify her non-mom friends, many Millennial Moms are emerging from the birth experience with an added bonus: a push present. Partners of expecting Millennials are aware of the push present early on, which is meant to be a gift from the father to signify his appreciation for his mama-to-be's dedication in carrying and delivering his offspring. While push presents have gotten a bad rap from its detractors (yes, all new moms recognize that the baby is a present in itself), plenty of others believe it's a sweet way for Daddy to say "Thanks" for all the not-so-fun side effects of pregnancy as well as "You rock" after witnessing the messy miracle of birth. Push presents can range from symbolic in nature (jewelry with the baby's birthstone) to more practical items (a fancy new camera to take endless infant pictures). Oftentimes they become a tangible reminder (aside from that new human they created) of a couple's journey into parenthood together.

*"I received a push present after the birth of my son, Max. While I was pregnant, the topic of push presents came up and my husband had never heard of the concept. I was happy to educate him on it and even though he didn't know that it was a 'thing,' he seemed to like the idea. Pregnancy wasn't easy for me (and neither was my labor!) and I think he liked being able to show his appreciation for the long road that led us to being parents — and the long road that lies ahead! His gift to me was a ring with our son's birthstone. Although I loved it, it didn't fit so we went together to exchange it for another setting. I ended up getting two stacking rings that feature my son's birthstone and my husband's. I love that it represents the two most important people in my life. I wear it every day and it's just as sentimental and meaningful to me as my engagement ring."—Lauren G., 28*

# #161 Babymoon before Baby On Board.

After months of hearing well-meaning friends (and sometimes strangers) tell them to "Stock up on sleep" and "Enjoy free time while you can," expectant Millennial couples are taking that advice to heart by taking one last vacation as a childless pair. Although one half of the duo might be carrying more weight, it's the perfect excuse to "travel light," sans strollers and Pack'n Plays, and escape for some quality couple time.

Babymoon destinations can range from beachfront resorts to mountain retreats and include activities like prenatal massages, leisurely strolls and gourmet dinners. Most babymoons are scheduled during the latter half of the second trimester or just into the third, so that Mom-to-be can enjoy herself without the aches and pains that arise later in pregnancy. While the focus is definitely on connecting with her partner, you might find a copy of *What to Expect* in her beach bag. With the weeks ticking by until she meets her little one, she's still stocking up on knowledge, as well as sleep.

*"My husband and I actually planned a babymoon prior to expecting. We decided to take 'one last trip' as a single couple before having children. We jetted off to Hawaii for a week of fun. We planned things this way so that we could spend time away from the hustle of work, life, etc., and just have time talking about our future. All while enjoying that 'one last memory' as just a couple as we relaxed on the beaches and snorkeled the waters. I cherish having this time with my husband and the memories because as much as we hope to enjoy Hawaii with both of our children one day, we also look back and remember that vacation of 'just us' to rekindle a bit of the spark between us. There are many great sites and guides out there that help in planning a babymoon getaway. I have referred a few friends to different places for ideas while planning their babymoon either while expecting or prior to. Places like Parenthood.com and TheBump.com offer great resources for trip tips and ideas. Plus, their communities are always buzzing with ideas. I think parenting sites do well in marketing this idea with tips and tricks to help parents decide when to go before baby and where to go. I also think local hotels would do well in offering babymoon packages, as some do in our area (Seattle). When couples choose to go just before baby is born, location and comfort are key! Being pregnant, you want to enjoy your vacation away but also perhaps be a little closer to home for the 'just in case' scenarios. Being someone who did travel while expecting, I would recommend bringing along the body pillow. Hotel beds are great, but I always slept with that wonderful invention for comfort."—Krystal C., 30*

*"I don't think companies do a great job marketing to the trend at all. If they did, they could offer mocktails, pregnancy massages and dinners that accommodate dietary requirements (remember how you can't eat certain cheeses and deli meats when pregnant).*

*Our big factor was a resort where we knew we could just stay on property and relax. Partially knowing that we would not be able to relax when the baby came but also to accommodate my waddling! I just wanted to minimize waddling everywhere. Lastly, staying in the U.S. was important due to healthcare. I think baby-moons have become a trend as life is very hectic. Most women are working through their pregnancies and after, so it is a time I think many people are taking for themselves and their partners. I also think many don't travel that first year with a baby (finances; babies are expensive), a hassle, not many places to accommodate babies (which BTW I was impressed with Beaches that did) and germ issues — so for this jet-setting generation it is one last chance to travel for the next two years probably."—Charlene D., 41*

*"For baby one, we decided to go back to the island where we honeymooned, Antigua. We honeymooned at Sandals but wanted a more subdued experience this time and chose Coco Bay Resort. It was definitely rustic and honestly didn't have the top-shelf drinks, etc., but that didn't matter to me obviously. I wanted peace and quiet and that was exactly what we had. We assumed it would be a while before we would take our kids to the Caribbean so it was a perfect choice for us. We also knew we wanted an adults-only experience. I think overall there are two kinds of babymoons to market to people. The first is the couples-only babymoon and the second would be a family babymoon. Celebrating a new sibling is a huge thing and I think it helped a ton that we did a family trip, just us three, before our family grew. It was really a special bonding time for us."— Melissa U., 39*

## #162 Monthly milestones give Millennial Moms a reason to celebrate.

The saying "The days are long but the years are short" is never more true than to the mom of an infant. And while mothers have for many years attempted to capture fleeting moments by taking and sharing baby photos, Millennial Moms have adopted a fun tradition for commemorating their baby's first year. Using fun onesie stickers or whimsical blocks, Millennial Moms mark the passing of each month of their child's life with a special photo, often taken in or near the same spot or position. These photos are typically shared via social media, sometimes accompanied with a fun profile of baby's current likes, dislikes and milestones. While most new moms carry out this exercise for 12 months only, some zealous mothers continue to mark their child's age in weeks and months well into toddlerhood — proof that to a Millennial, no milestone is too small to be celebrated.

## #163 Flaunting the baby bump.

Boomer and even Gen X moms kept their bumps hidden under lacy tunic dresses and oversized shirts, but not so for their Millennial daughters. The Millennial Mom is proud of her baby bump and she documents the growth of it every month on Facebook. You may have seen them: a cute 20-something standing in front of a mirror, with a numerical sticker on her tummy, taking a selfie. Month after month, she documents the progress of her pregnancy and shares it with friends and family. For marketers there's an opportunity to join her in the celebration.

### #TakeNote

If you see your customers posting a baby bump photo, it's acceptable and even welcome to leave a congratulatory comment. Or if you have a product that is perfect for her stage of pregnancy, it's fine to message her with a product sample or coupon offer. The personal and intimate communication will go a long way toward establishing a long-term relationship.

## #164 Hey dude!

Traditionally, expectant moms and their growing bumps have been the center of attention at baby showers. With Millennial Dads being more involved in all aspects of parenting, it's not surprising that dads want a special shower-like event, too! Whether you call them "man showers" or "dadchelor parties," dads are celebrating their entry into fatherhood with their friends by hosting these casual events in places like their living rooms or at their favorite bars. For men, these parties aren't about cute onesies and crocheted blankets, but about male bonding, friendship and, quite often, beer. Dads typically receive simple gifts like diapers, wipes and gift cards, along with plenty of advice from other dads. These celebrations allow dads to receive much-deserved recognition for their journey into fatherhood.

# CHAPTER
# 9

## Family Life

# #165 Millennials live in a concierge economy.

There are apps for everything from doing your laundry to having a doctor make house calls. If they find value in the service, they will pay for it. It's "Uber" everything.

**Popular Concierge Apps Among Millennial Moms**

| Luxe | Push for Pizza | Washio |
| Lyft | Sprig | Zeel |
| One Medical | Saucey | |
| Postmates | Uber | |

# #166 No minivans for this generation of moms.

Not only has her selection of family vehicles changed from the "mom-mobile" her mother drove, she is purchasing cars differently. According to J.D. Powers & Associates, Millennials account for only 27% of new car purchases in 2014. They tend to be more frugal and purchase used vehicles in lieu of large monthly payments.

**Popular Family Vehicles**

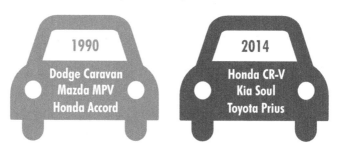

**1990**
Dodge Caravan
Mazda MPV
Honda Accord

**2014**
Honda CR-V
Kia Soul
Toyota Prius

# #167 She's not afraid to take "me time" away from the family.

I'm not going to tell you that she feels less guilt than her predecessor, but Millennial Moms find more time to get away with friends and her spouse, with 68% saying they get together with friends face-to-face at least a few times a month. Of these, 23% say they socialize with friends a few times a week. These numbers are slightly higher than those of Generation X moms and considerably higher than those of Boomer mothers, who perhaps were staying home and doting on their Millennial children.

Relationships, as we all know, are important to Millennials and it shows in the frequency of date nights. Over 79% of moms said they go out with their spouse or partner at least once a week. With the increase in moms who enjoy spending time with other moms it should come as no surprise that events such as National Mom's Nite Out™ (www.momsniteout.com) continue to grow. The event, which I created with my team at BSM Media, takes place on the Thursday night before Mother's Day each year and attracts millions of mothers around the globe while providing yet another occasion to put the Millennial Mom in the spotlight.

*"Making time for ourselves is something that all women struggle with, regardless of age. Women have a tendency to put themselves last, often going days or even weeks without taking an extended period of time for their own self-care. One of the big reasons that women struggle with this is comparison, and I think social media breeds comparison for Millennials in particular. They read blogs, follow people on Instagram, see Facebook status updates and compare their own lives to those postings. Feelings of what they 'should' be doing creep in because of what they see and read online. These emotions then prevent them from making time for their passions."—Jessica T., 32*

*"Honestly, I don't take 'me time' as often as I should. I know it's important for my stress levels. I feel like I'm a better mom after I've had some time to just relax and be less 'mom' and more just the woman I was before I had kids. I like to go shopping (and not the grocery variety), get lunch, or see a movie. Just something that doesn't require much planning or thought. The best 'me time' for me is low-key and stress free! It leaves me feeling refreshed and usually missing my kids by the end of my time to myself!"—Mariah M., 30*

*"Once I saw your question I was searching for a way to say 'no, I don't feel guilty' when I take 'me time,' but the truth is, I do. Me time usually occurs during the day when the little ones are in school and my husband is at work. During this time I schedule lunch with other mom friends, go shopping and sometimes I go*

*wine tasting. I need this time to reset, as being a mom is hard work. I feel I'd be far less tolerant and efficient if my soul wasn't fully charged."—Maggie S., 33*

*"I do take 'me time' and NOW I don't feel guilty about it. Mostly because I have more than one child and a great support system. 'Me time' gives me the opportunity to focus on my needs so I can better fulfill the needs of my husband and children. It also keeps them knowledgeable of the fact that I won't always be around to solve problems for them. My husband and I established early on that while we're out, no phone calls except for emergencies. It helps to make us feel like our alone time is respected. I'm sure I'd be way more frazzled if I didn't get 'me time' or if I didn't have a husband who understood the NEED and importance of it."—Natasha N., 34*

### Things Moms Love To Do To Relax

Reading **86%**  Cooking **50%**  Exercising **43%**  Outdoor Activity **41%**

Crafting **41%**  Photography **33%**  Scrapbooking **27%**  Sewing/Knitting **27%**

Spa Time **26%**  Writing **24%**  Blogging **23%**  Play Instrument **10%**

# #168 "Me time" is used on passions.

Jessica N. Turner, author of *The Fringe Hours*, took a deep look at women, their passions and their use of "me time." If you're interested in this topic, I highly recommend her site, www.fringehours.com. She surveyed more than 2,000 women and shared her research with me while I was writing this book. We asked almost identical questions about moms and downtime. I was as thrilled, as any researcher would be, that our results were very closely aligned. Turner asked respondents to tell her what they loved to do when they had time to themselves. She did a nice job illustrating the results. I've shared them below.

# #169 Millennial Moms don't wear "mom jeans."

It's called "athleisure" and you have likely seen it on Millennial Moms both in the office and at the grocery store. It's casual leggings and comfortable tops that can transition from work to play. It's about efficiency and comfort, but found at upscale retailers like Lululemon and Bloomingdale's. Fashion experts believe that athleisure is here to stay as FitBit and Apple Watch become the jewelry statement and flywheel spin classes and yoga continue to grow.

# #170 Millennials are likely to own pets before having children.

Call them Pet Parents: the Millennial couples who test their parenting skills with a family pet before a baby arrives. According to the American Pet Products Association, the majority of new pets last year went to Millennials. Many of the same attributes marketers see in their behaviors around spending on children are emulated in the attention they give to their household pets.

Millennials are willing to splurge on their pets, seeking the latest technology that enhances experiences with their pets and purchasing brands tied to causes they believe in.[1] According to our BSM Media survey of Millennial Moms, 35% spend more than $50 monthly on their family pet. Another 29% spend over $51 each month. And you might not be surprised to learn that they select products for their pets in much the same way they decide on products for their children. They buy based on quality, value and product reviews. In fact, 85% of Millennial Moms said they use the same research methods for pet items as they use for items for their children.

Almost 40% of moms say they celebrate a pet's birthday just as they would a child's and when it comes to following pet brands on social media, it's most common that they follow them on Facebook followed by Twitter and Instagram. Marketing to the pet owner is very aligned with the techniques used in marketing to moms, so for that reason we often invite brands with a pet focus to join us in marketing to moms.

## #171 The role of the dad has changed for Millennial couples.

I've focused up to now on the influence that Boomer parents had on Millennial Moms. However, the same parenting patterns have had an effect on Millennial Dads, too. They were raised to believe they could achieve anything and fortunately for today's moms, this includes conquering the tasks of diapering a baby, laundry and cooking. Apparently they don't mind seizing the opportunity to be more involved in raising their children. The number of stay-at-home fathers in the U.S. has tripled in the past 10 years — up to 154,000, according to the most recent census (although not all by choice due to the recession). Some experts argue that the real figure could actually be in the millions, if the definition is broadened to include dads who work part-time while remaining the primary caregivers.[2]

## #172 Millennial Dads blog to feel engaged with parenthood.

So much has been written about the participation of dads and the growth of Dad Blogs. What motivates a dad to start a blog?

*"I started my blog because there was a ton of mom blogs but few dad blogs that shared my voice or thoughts on the topic of fatherhood. Since I started six years ago that landscape has changed — there are thousands of dad blogs now, and I think that shows the shift in fatherhood. Millennial Dads want to be engaged fathers, they look for work- life balance, they look to be more than just a provider but they want to be today's dad. At first I started blogging*

*because I wanted to share my story, then it became about the community of dads, and now I'm just hooked between the perks that it offers, the emails that say thanks for blogging from a dad's point of view, and the great friends and community of the dad blog world."—Adam C., 34*

## #173 Millennial Moms read Millennial Dad blogs, too.

*"I do read dad blogs. I find that dads have a totally different hand than moms. Their outlook and insight gives me a view from the male perspective. Both are equally beneficial because another viewpoint can shine a light you may not see without it."—Amanda H., 35*

*"I read dad blogs! They provide various viewpoints, different interests, and I love reading what they think is important! Most of the dad bloggers I read/follow socially are creative, funny or downright open about what they talk about. While you will always find a mom blogger that may be able to fit that same specs, there's something different about the male species that allows dad blogs to bring something different to the table."—Lindsey P., 34*

## #174 What do you do as a dad that's different than your own dad?

Millennial Dads are much more involved in their children's lives and more active in sharing household responsibilities. Whereas previous generations saw Dad's role as that of the traditional breadwinner, financial planner and often the disciplinarian, this generation has an expectation that fathers will be more active in family life. Roles are often shared and also switched, as one mom summarizes: "My husband is so involved — working opposite shifts so one of us can always be with them. We each have our role. He does a.m. and I do p.m. parenting. On weekends everything is shared."

The overwhelming response in our survey indicates that moms see today's dads as "much more hands-on and involved." Dads do more around the home and have no qualms about manning up to help with children.

*"They are willing to be more involved in raising children, taking a lot of responsibilities that mainly the moms would do."—Sarah, 31*

*"My Dad was a great guy; he tried to be at every major event but still it was a focus between work and life and sometimes that work life balanced more towards work. I always balance more towards family. I have accepted positions for less salary because I know it would give me more time at home. I think there was more focus on the one with the most cash wins, where our generation values time over money."*—Adam C., 34

# #175 Traveling with the Millennial is a different experience.

From Starbucks in the lobby to free Wi-Fi access on property, we can thank the rapidly growing group of Millennial travelers for a huge shift in how hoteliers, both large and boutique, are wooing guests. Hotel owners and the travel industry in general are adjusting to meet the needs of what the 2013 Portrait of Digital Travelers™ calls "The Digital Elite." This report by the MMGY Global/Harrison Group identifies this cohort as "individuals who own and use at least two digital devices (a smartphone and tablet) to plan and purchase travel services. This segment has grown from five percent of all active travelers in 2011 to fully one third (33%) today, an increase of over 600 percent." These travelers also average more trips per year, including "staycations" and last-minute trips, outspending less connected travelers by almost $1,200 annually.

With this younger generation of travelers in mind, global mega-chain Marriott is undergoing a large-scale rollout of new hotel rooms and public spaces. Under the Moxy brand, the new look features downsized rooms (averaging 200 square feet of sleeping space) and upgraded public spaces with free Wi-Fi and all-night cafes.[3]

Other hotels — from large chains to small, independent and boutique lodgings — are undergoing similar renovations to capture the Millennials' travel dollars, with the idea that earning the business of the young, budget-minded traveler will build a loyal relationship as this generation travels for work or vacations later in life.

# #176 Millennials Moms live and operate in a shared economy.

Of course, no discussion would be complete without mentioning Airbnb and Uber, travel and transportation concepts that have turned their respective industries inside out, thanks to Millennials and their beliefs in a shared economy.

In this fact, the word "shared" takes on two very distinct, but related definitions for Millennials. A shared or collaborative economy is eagerly embraced by Millennials, as witnessed by industry-changing companies like Airbnb and Uber that each have only a few years of history but an expected annual profit in 2015 of $20 billion and $10 billion respectively, according to a BusinessInsider.com blog. Millennials are driving this economic concept in which individuals are able to borrow or rent assets owned by someone else, with participation nearly doubling from 2013 to 2014 — a trend that's expected to only keep growing.[1] Millennial Moms are sharing everything from garden space to grow their own vegetables to babysitters for a night out. They're sharing not only their skills to earn a few extra dollars but also bartering with other moms to get the most out of their products and their income. It's not uncommon for them to share their time by having one mom run errands in exchange for the other mom cooking a family dinner for her. If one mom bakes she might exchange fresh cookies for a casserole another mother stirs up. Mothers are sharing their talents as well. Sixty percent of moms with a child at home under the age of six earns some kind of income by working for another mother —perhaps answering emails, writing blog posts as a contributing author or supporting an Etsy business.

Of course, the other definition for "shared" is what drives the success of these businesses mentioned above. Shared reviews and ratings are critical to the success of hosts and vendors, from a driver in Miami to a one-bed accommodation in Barcelona. Airbnb, Yelp, Uber and others like them are counting on the Millennials' love of sharing and 24/7 access through smartphones and apps to continue pushing the envelope of economic change.

The shared economy of the Millennial Mom is an important

concept to understand. It presents in some cases new opportunities for product and service providers. There could be a time when moms shop together to maximize bulk purchases or a time when Millennials hire other mothers to do their grocery shopping. These may seem like crazy ideas; however, did we ever think we'd see a day when moms would buy a soda because the word "Mom" was on the bottle of Coke? If we've learned anything from Millennials, it's that anything's possible.

# #177 Millennials consume news differently than prior generations.

Prior generations consumed news in sessions, like the nightly news or a constant flow of CNN throughout the day. The Millennial, however, acquires news while socializing online. It's a mixed flow of hard news and lifestyle stories and Facebook is the biggest leader to the full story.[4] It may surprise you to learn that YouTube is the next largest source of social news and most likely the reason Hillary Clinton announced her presidential candidacy on this social media platform. Twitter acts as a source for breaking news and trending topics. You may recall that the death of Bin Laden and Egyptian unrest both broke first on Twitter. The Millennial is interested in global and local news; she just consumes it through different channels than prior generations.

# CHAPTER
# 10

## Food

# #178 Food takes on new meaning and evokes new interactions for Millennial Moms.

From the generation that coined the term "foodie," it's no surprise that the Millennial generation is redefining all things food and dining. They have challenged fast-food giants with their desire for fresh, fast casual dining and demand for WiFi-enabled dining areas. Millennial Moms are changing the way restaurants as well as grocery retailers compete for market share. Millennials demand new flavors and are willing to try any recipe once. Recently, I overheard two Millennial Moms talking about their dinner plans for after work. As they compared, one of them said, "I just look for the recipes online that have the most comments and experiment with that to make it my own." Millennial Moms are adventurous when it comes to food and they want brands to give them ways to discover their products.

# #179 Apps replace magazines for recipe sources.

You might be surprised to find out why. Because magazines don't have reviews. They might have glossy pictures that most women admire, but that doesn't work for the Millennial Mom. She wants to see reviews. One Millennial Mom told me recently, "I won't cook anything that doesn't have at least three stars. Most of the time it has to be four or five stars and I want to see the variations others have made with the recipe." Another mother explained during the same discussion, "I only cook the number-one recipes with the most reviews because then I can be assured that it's the best banana bread. If eight hundred other people baked it and it was great, I know it will be good for me."

### Top Recipe Apps According to Millennials

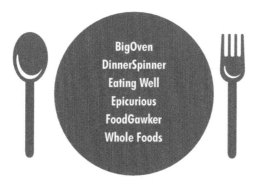

BigOven
DinnerSpinner
Eating Well
Epicurious
FoodGawker
Whole Foods

# #180 After her children, food is one of her top photo subject matters.

"I LOVE food photos! I'm a very visual person so when I see a tasty recipe on Instagram or Facebook, I almost always message or look for the recipe and I share for the exact same reason. Plus my kids are #foodiekids, so we're always on the prowl for new things to try. Oh and a good food shot (to me) are the ones that provoke an emotion from me. Like a beautiful salad placed next to a cold glass of fruit-infused water with an amazing sunset in the background! It makes me want that salad AND that experience."—Chene W., 33

"A friend of mine posted a pic of biscotti that she made. I don't even like biscotti (I might not even know how to spell it right), but I feel like making it. My Facebook friends really do influence my decisions."—Eva W., 34

"Food photos bring you memories plus also give you ideas to present your dishes differently. Great for inspiration! Also, I have purchased ingredients or tools after seeing them used on blogs or Instagram."—Jeanette K., 35

"Learning is one of the reasons that I like food images. I'm a foodie and love to get ideas as far as presentation, recipes and seasonal ingredients. I've been able to create new dishes at home from things I've found online or via Pinterest. Especially those easy to do meals or drinks for moms on the go and family events."—Dee T., 30

# #181 Family dinner has a new definition.

Mealtime is one of the biggest challenges for moms regardless of their generation or the age of her child. There is a universal sigh that echoes throughout the world of moms when someone asks, "What's for dinner?" The challenges of mealtime, however, go beyond food. For decades, the media has broadcasted the importance of the family dinner as a preventative measure against drug abuse and divorce as well as a key indicator to academic success. But the Millennial Mom doesn't have to be convinced of the benefit of family dinners. In fact, it's one of the elements of her own childhood that she most desires to replicate in her own family. It's such a priority for her that she has redefined what the family dinner looks like.

Overwhelmingly, in several surveys conducted by BSM Media this year, Millennial Moms told us that a family dinner is a meal where at least part of the family is together. Notice I didn't mention where they were sitting? That's because the Millennial Mom doesn't care where they are, as long as they are together. A family dinner can be Family Night at Chick-fil-A when Dad is working late, or it can be at the kitchen counter eating with just one of her children. The key component of the family dinner for the Millennial Mom is that she is bonding and connecting with at least one member of her immediate family. The "what" she's serving is always an interesting element for food brands or meal providers. Although they love to search out new recipes on Pinterest, Millennial Moms don't require a meal cooked from scratch to label it a family dinner. In fact, we found that 55% of mothers will doctor up a store-bought roasted chicken or a premade pizza with homemade salads and call it a home-cooked meal. The meal is not as important as the company she keeps around the table.

BSM Media has done extensive research in the area of family meals and meal planning over the years. While we're focused on dinnertime, I'd like to share some of it with you. Among other challenges that moms claim as an obstacle to meal planning are cleanup time, ability to serve during staggered arrivals to the table and broad appeal for the whole family. Price plays a part in eating out but variety is equally important to her. Eighty-two percent of mothers want to be able to serve prepared, store-bought and delivered meals on her timetable, so the ability to reheat and re-serve foods is helpful to her family's schedule. She wants fresh for her family, which means vegetables, fruits and a reduction in processed foods. Millennial Moms in particular appreciate apps that help her order ahead, like Chipotle's. When it comes to takeout foods, 60% of moms purchase them multiple times a year for larger gatherings like school events and family gatherings. It's important to remember the Millennial Mom in your catering marketing as well. Millennial Moms find dinner ideas on Pinterest, as well as on blogs and via family members. Finally, my favorite statistic of all time: at 3 pm, 65% of moms do not know what they are cooking for dinner. If you are a food provider, this is your target time to be on email, Pinterest, Facebook and Instagram. She's looking for you!

## #182 Millennials Moms seek healthy fast-food options.

From fast food to farm-to-table restaurants, Millennials are changing the restaurant landscape. Fast food still has a place in a mom's busy schedule, but the options have changed dramatically in the last few years with the emergence of fast casual restaurants. "Fresh," "integrity" and "ethical" are some of the keywords that resonate with Millennials and explain the booming business of fast casual restaurants like Chipotle and Moe's. Chipotle boasted a 56% increase in sales in 2014 with market share among Millennials at twice the number of other generations.[1]

McDonald's, the fast-food grandparent, has seen their share of customers in the 19-to-21-year-old age bracket fall almost 13% since 2011.[2] McDonald's has even lost hold of the child market as Chick-fil-A has exceeded them in 2014 sales with their fresh options for kids' meals.

## #183 Millennial Moms are interested in eating local; farm-to-table dining options continue to grow.

Restaurants are rushing to find the right mixes of flavor, local and healthy in order to tap into the lucrative Millennial market. Regardless of income, Millennials dine at restaurants more often than other generations, at a rate of 3.4 times weekly compared to 2.8 for other groups.[3] As illustrated in Fact #178, the desire for healthy fast food spawned the introduction of the "fast casual" category of restaurants such as Chipotle, Panera Bread and Panda Express, along with the popular farm-to-table category.

# #184 Healthy comes at a price for Millennial Moms, one they sometimes can't afford.

As the primary grocery shopper in close to two-thirds of U.S. households, Millennial Moms are much more conscious of what they and their families are eating at home. However, the desire for healthy, natural and organic food often comes at a price that many Millennials find too high. The rapid growth of small organic and natural stores, as well as larger retailers like Whole Foods Market, The Fresh Market and Trader Joe's, are a direct result of the Millennial generation's focus on healthier, 'cleaner' eating. However, the affordability of these foods can be a challenge. To cash in on the Millennials' desire for organic and natural foods at more reasonable prices, Whole Foods recently rolled out their 365 Everyday Value brand. Many grocers are following suit by introducing more affordable store brands that resonate with Millennials and their desire for healthy, more natural foods for their families.

# #185 Millennial Moms read labels.

Unlike some of their older counterparts, these moms use technology to research products and the ingredients in them. Label-reading is more common with the Millennial Mom as she seeks the most nutritious, 'clean' products for her family. She's seeking authentic food options and this research-savvy mom knows that she can find it by reading about the ingredients. Diets such as Paleo and The Whole30 keep her focused on what's in the food she's putting into her body and on the dinner table for her family.

# #186 Her children's lunches look more like a bento box than a brown-bag meal.

What child doesn't remember eating a soggy peanut butter and jelly sandwich as part of a lunch their mom made them for school? Well, it's likely that some of the children of Millennial Moms will never experience one. Their memories will include bento boxes of themed foods cut in small shapes and mixed with new flavors like kale, passionfruit and mango. Thanks to hundreds of lunchbox blogs and Pinterest, Millennial Moms have plenty of creative thought-starters when it comes to their children's lunchboxes. She enjoys the challenge, and doing something special for her child helps her to feel more connected with him/her. This trend opens the door for brands and products that perhaps have never seen the inside of a brown bag. Marketers should take a step back and see how packaging modifications and flavor enhancements might put your product in a new category. Who knows? Maybe soy chips could take the place of Twinkies for the next generation.

## #TakeNote

Think of using Pinterest and Facebook to provide moms with ways to present your food products to her family. It's time to think beyond just cutting sandwiches into shapes. Push your test kitchens to discover new flavor combinations she can put together at home. Do some social listening to see how she might be using your product already. You're likely to find those ideas on Pinterest or on blogs such as Lunchboxdad.com. Also remember that small is the new super-size when it comes to food for Millennials. Consider repackaging your food to mini-sizes that give Mom the opportunity to "stash and go" in lunches, sports bags and purses.

## #187 Millennials are influencing online grocery options.

The $600 billion U.S. grocery industry has been largely unaffected by e-commerce — until recently. A 2014 *Business Insider* tech report notes that shopping habits are changing with the development of niche online grocery services focused on convenience and selection, two priorities that define Millennials. In fact, 25% of Millennials say they would pay a premium for same-day delivery of groceries, more than any other generation noted in the report. The industry is counting on this customized approach as a 21% annual growth in online grocery sales is predicted over the next three years (compared to 3.1% growth in offline grocery totals). Again, it's Uber-everything and Millennials will spur the advent of customized purchasing and delivery options that will change an industry.

*Reward Millennial Moms when they least expect it, and it reminds these moms that you are striving for a relationship for the long haul.*

# Brand Relationships

# #188 It's time for brands to learn how to listen.

The confident Millennial Mom not only wants respect as I discussed in Fact #21, but she wants to be heard. As a child she received trophies for participating in sports, clubs and groups. Her mother taught her that showing up and contributing was as important, if not more important, than winning. Now that she's an adult, she applies a childhood of participation by commenting and contributing to conversations. And thanks to also being told by her mother that she has the potential to accomplish great things, she believes she has something of value to say. She has a point to make and she wants you to listen.

This is a very big concept. In fact, if given the time and audience, I could speak on this one subject for hours. Listening is the number-one most important tactic of marketing and it's more important today than it has ever been with any other generation of mothers. Fortunately the need for listening comes with the availability of technology to make your job easier.

For the more socially engaged Millennial Moms, you can listen to their online conversations by following keywords. We do it every morning in our offices for clients. I'll give you an example. We represent a children's probiotic company, BioGaia. For mothers, it offers practical, natural relief for tummy aches or constipation during potty training. Every morning we search a list of 12 words/terms that relate to the problems BioGaia can help alleviate for mothers. They include "potty training," "vomit," "upset stomach," "constipation" and more — you get the idea. When we find the related tweets by moms, we view the online conversations around these topics. This practice allows us to not only gain insights on how moms are speaking to each other about potty training and treating upset stomachs, but BioGaia also learns to have a more meaningful response to the mother's tweet. Listen. Too often brands want to jump into a social platform headfirst, bringing all their promotional messages along with them. It's not the right approach with the Millennial Mom who wants a two-way relationship.

# #189 Listen to conversations where moms are posting.

We see Millennial Moms' desire to be heard in the review and comment forums that exist on Amazon, TripAdvisor, Yelp and many other popular websites. This is another opportunity to practice your listening skills. The comment and review threads offer rich insights on how the Millennial Mom not only feels about your product but about your competitors as well. When was the last time you read the reviews for products that are similar to your own? How often do your read your own comments on Amazon? Most important, how often do you thank a mom for posting a positive review on Yelp?

It's so easy for a brand to express their appreciation by liking a comment or posting a response to the comment. It not only shows the mom who is posting that you share her desire for a relationship, but it demonstrates to the other moms who consult the review that you are a brand that wants to be connected with your customers. It's a win-win situation for everyone involved.

# #190 Millennial Moms don't want to call your customer service line.

She values customer service but she doesn't want to talk to you on the phone. Forty-seven percent of Millennial Moms want to communicate with brands by email. Online chat is also a preferred method of service. Less than 15% of Millennials and only 19% of Generation X mothers want to call and speak to a live customer-service agent. If you really want to drive these two cohorts of moms away, send her to an automated response system. Less than 1% of both groups want an automated response from companies. Customer-service reps need to be empowered to help the Millennial Mom make changes or find a solution. Remember, this mom wants immediate gratification and seeks a sense of accomplishment. Waiting to speak to you on a phone line does not achieve this for her.

Older Millennials are more patient than younger Millennials. The younger Millennials expect online issues to be resolved with 30 minutes, while older Millennials will wait a few hours. Millennials feel that customer service and social media are one and the same — which is quite different from how many organizations are structured, with customer service often a part of operations and social media a function of marketing. It seems appropriate to also mention the Millennial Moms' uses of Twitter and Facebook to gain resolution to problems. Within the blogosphere in particular, it's a common practice for moms to Tweet to brands when they have a problem. Brands such as Zappos, Comcast and JetBlue have done a good job developing a reputation for being responsive to tweets. Comcast, I think, has taken the best strategy. They created a team of Comcast personae on Twitter; it gives you the feeling that you're talking to a concerned friend. Next time the cable goes out, try tweeting @ComcastCares and see what I mean. You can thank me later.

Another example of good Millennial customer service is Sephora. They have many ways to reach out: Instagram, Twitter, Facebook and an online forum called "Beauty Talk." In the forum you can get answers from both users and Sephora moderators. They respond to Facebook messages within 2 – 3 hours.

## #TakeNote

Typically, traditional business models have marketing and customer-service teams in separate operation centers, resulting in inconsistent communication at best. These two teams need to be more closely aligned because customer service is so important when marketing to Millennial Moms. Any strategic plan to capture the Millennial Mom market must include strong customer-service tactics in order to be successful.

## #191 Brand loyalty as defined by Millennial Moms.

"I've recently found myself becoming loyal to brands that reach out to online influencers to promote their products. For example, Neutrogena and Colgate recently used some of my favorite You-Tubers for nationwide commercials. I trust this relationship because I've seen these YouTubers mention in their vlogs that they use those products every day. Instead of looking to celebrities for endorsements of brands, Millennials are looking at their favorite online influencers. We understand that loyalty and partnership is built off the

*passion that the influencer had before a monetary*
*was created."—Amiyrah M., 33*

"*Chevy — growing up my family had a loyalty to*
*my grandfather sold Chevys. The fact that they are Ameri*
*also has impacted that loyalty. Not only are they reliable a*
*vehicles, they are beyond safe. I will time and time again c*
*to be loyal to Chevy BC of a car accident that I was in when I was*
*20. I should have died but because of the car I survived. Disney —*
*anything and everything Disney. Nostalgia, memories and the fact*
*that they always exceed expectations for us is why we will be beyond*
*loyal. From the parks, to the movies, to TV shows, we eat, sleep,*
*and breathe Disney. As a child I remember watching The Wonderful*
*World of Disney with my parents and grandparents. Today I watch*
*it as well as Disney Channel Junior with my child. It is a staple in*
*our house and has been a part of her DNA."—Jennifer G., 33*

# #192 A nice photo on Pinterest will win you a Millennial's click.

I've already discussed how influential Pinterest is in the purchasing process of a Millennial Mom. I want to dig deeper, however, to uncover what it is about the pictures on Pinterest that will trigger a sale. When I asked Millennial Moms about how an image influences her buying decision, the responses fell into several themes. First, the image itself. They like eye-catching pictures that convey the quality of the product. Millennial Moms also like pictures that show the product being used in some way. They want to see how it works and how they can use it to benefit their family. The second theme focused on who was using the product. Moms like to see moms they know using the product. Even if they don't personally know them, if it's a mother they know on social media, they will think twice about trying it. Finally and most important, they want to see comments and reviews of the product attached to the image. A few positive comments under a Pinterest picture can be the determining factor on whether a mom buys the product now or moves on to another one. Pinterest is a powerful marketing tool that is often underutilized by brands that are overwhelmed by maintaining social media.

If Millennial Moms are your target, I would suggest putting Pinterest at the top of your social-media priority list.

*"Pinterest is all about visual imagery, so first and foremost the photography has to be good. A gorgeous photo really encourages me to click over, as does something informational (like '10 tips for keeping the house clean' or '10 must-do things at Disney World,' etc). And vertical images always capture my eye more (because they take up more room on Pinterest)."—Sara W., 27*

## #193 Millennial Moms aren't seeing themselves in marketing images.

I first asked moms in 2001 if they believed marketers were accurately portraying them in ads and have done so nearly every year since then. In 2002, 80% of moms said that marketers did a poor job of representing them — as compared to only 65% agreeing to the same today. Although some progress has been made, there is still plenty of room for improvement.

*"Typically moms represented in advertising tend to fall into two categories: the perfect 'Stepford' wife and mom or the crazed caricature of an exhausted mom who needs a break. In both of those scenarios, the moms pictured tend to look slightly older than how I see myself and it's challenging to relate to either depiction. When brands try too hard to relate to the 'cool' mom, the results aren't always what they are aiming for. The recent Hefty Ultimate cups ads show moms as closet party animals, spouting off teen slang. While I can see the direction the brand was trying to go, the spots just seem awkward and it certainly doesn't make me want to go out and purchase the cups they are pushing. I think the brand I've seen that comes closest to relating to my sense of self is Dove. Although the ads aren't geared towards moms specifically, the messages of self love and individuality are ones that all women can embrace and the fact that they show people of all races and sizes is refreshing without trying too hard."—Amy S., 29*

*"I do and I don't. The one thing I struggle with are some of the really expensive product lines and brands out there. I'm a stay-at-home Mom, so we aren't a two-income family who can afford to pay $1200 for a stroller — no matter how awesome it is. I love*

*companies like Graco who promote why they are awesome, the great features they have and how they are still affordable for most families. Affordability is huge in this house. Again, they are also a company willing to work with influencers through doing giveaways and reviews, showing they care about their customers."—Carolyn B., 35*

# #194 Eliminate the small talk when it's a call to action.

Millennial Moms like to get down to business quickly. Keep this in mind when designing your marketing and advertising. Remember how the Millennial Mom was raised with clear expectations and a trophy for doing what was expected. She wants to know your call to action so don't forget to have it front and center in all communications with her.

# #195 Conversations with Millennial Moms are an advertiser's best tool.

In Fact #24, I described the value that Millennial Moms put on relationships — including relationships with brands. The best way to initiate and deepen a relationship with a Millennial Mom is through a meaningful and relevant conversation. Thanks to social media, the dialogue with mothers is easier than ever. Brands don't always have to be the first to shake hands; there is the opportunity to respond to things she posts on Facebook or to an image she shares on Instagram. Companies no longer have to be wallflowers standing in the corner waiting to be asked to join the dialogue. You should approach each mom who engages with you as a potential partner with the ability to amplify your messages over a long period of time. Keep track of the moms you engage with and make sure that you return to them when you can offer exclusive perks or product previews. Reward them when they least expect it and it reminds these moms that you are striving for a relationship for the long haul. There are several ways to maintain the conversation with select moms including email lists, private Facebook groups of superfans or Twitter lists. Whatever the means, ensure that the conversation is constant and valuable to the mom and she will reward you with loyalty.

# #196 What does a "like" on Facebook mean to you?

Millennial Moms show their favor (or disfavor) through social media. When moms like a brand, almost 90% will "like" them on Facebook, 60% will follow their Twitter account and 48% will follow their Instagram account. More traditional methods are still popular: 59% say they will join a company's mailing list while 70% will visit the website.

*"When I like a brand on Facebook it is because I want to keep up to date with the product they are putting out, and/or keep up with any special offers."— Amy, 30*

# #197 Brands hitting a home run with Millennial Moms.

Almost 75% of Millennial Moms in our survey agree that companies target them as a specific consumer group. Cleaning, dieting, and health and beauty products lead the category list of mom-specific outreach, with the most common mentions of companies including Tide, Johnson & Johnson, Pampers, Burt's Bees, Fisher-Price and Target, indicating that these companies are doing it well.

*"The brands that stick out to me in regard to marketing to Moms are Fisher Price and Disney. They seem to know their market well in regard to who is spending the money in the family and what it is that we Moms want to remember about our lives with young kids. They focus on memories and experiences all while tying in the product they are trying to sell. They're willing to put what they want to sell right into the hands of Moms by working with social media influencers who then share it with their other Mom friends. It's genius and it works. I think a lot of brands are greatly missing the mark by simply pushing product and not the experience. Storytelling is huge."—Carolyn B., 35*

# #198 Millennial Moms aren't afraid to publicly shame a company that treats them poorly.

It's a company's worst nightmare: a mom shares a bad experience with another mom. Today, however, thanks to social media, that sharing of a bad experience can mean thousands of other moms. This is why I encourage brands to constantly monitor not only their social media pages but also social media platforms in general. Pay attention to hashtags attached to your brand, even if you didn't create them, and search your product name frequently on Twitter and Instagram. How you respond is important to turning the situation around — but if you never find the comment, you can't respond. Here are a few helpful tips on handling this unfavorable situation. First, monitor social media as I just mentioned. The socially savvy Millennial Mom will want to ensure you see her comment so she is likely to @you on Twitter or use a hashtag reflective of your company. Second, apologize publicly for the benefit of other moms who read her post. Moms know things happen and they respect the brand that admits when they are wrong. Third, attempt to reach out to her privately via some type of social media channel. I'll give you a personal experience with a brand that, after an unpleasant shopping experience, wowed me because of the way they responded.

The retailer is Mattress Firm. I was desperate for a mattress for my daughter and ran in to purchase a mattress only to find out that you can't actually buy a mattress and leave with it the same day. The whole concept of not being able to pay for a mattress and take it home with me blew me away. I might be a Boomer but I act like a Millennial — instant gratification is a must. After hearing all the reasons that I couldn't take the product home with me, I sent out a tweet from @MomTalkRadio: *@MattressFirm I will never shop in your store again because you sell mattress I can't buy.* The next morning I arrived at my office to hear my phone ringing. It was the social media manager of Mattress Firm. She was calling to see how they could win back my business. I was shocked and quite impressed. I explained nicely that I probably wouldn't go back to her store but I would send out a more flattering tweet about their brand. It was nice to see a brand take the time to find me online and I felt compelled to acknowledge their excellent level of customer service. My story is not an anomaly. Almost daily I see a post, tweet or video calling out a brand for bad service. Being proactive is the best way to avoid a customer-service catastrophe.

# #199 Millennials read emails in the morning rather than at night.

This is quite different from the Gen Xers and Boomers who typically relax at night reading emails from 8 – 10 pm. It was a trend with these two generations to co-view television with their laptops open. The Millennial instead browses Pinterest and shopping sites at night, leaving productivity for her daytime hours. This means for marketers that it's best to set your Constant Contact or email systems so that your promotional emails are sent first thing in the morning and are at the top of her inbox rather than the bottom.

# #200 Moms are more likely to select a brand that is active on social media.

Millennial Moms love social media and it shows in how they choose their brands. Almost 25% say they are "most likely" and 28% are "very likely" to favor a brand with a presence on social media. In the same Annalect report cited in Fact #186, more than half of Millennials, 52%, say the technology a brand uses is the strongest influence when making a purchase.

## #TakeNote

Just as you would do a budgetary audit on a regular basis, it's time to do a social media audit to make sure your brand has a presence on the newest social media platforms. It's simple to do: ask moms what is the latest and greatest social media tool.

# #201 Millennial Moms like brands that make her feel good about herself.

Brands that earn the loyalty of a Millennial Mom do so through authentic, transparent and realistic messages. In order to give you a broad and honest look into how Millennials feel about specific brands, we presented an open-ended question with the promise of anonymity to the moms in our network. In the following quotes, you will see the responses about specific brands that are doing it right and others that are missing the target when it comes to marketing to Millennial Moms.

*"The Limited and Francesca's both follow and like most of my pictures and always comment the nicest things!"*

*"Brands that interact and are helpful are nice."*

*"Eco-friendly brands that are transparent about their practices."*

*"Dove, Aveda, Johnson's & Johnson's make me feel good about myself. The way they promote positive images around women, and mothers is uplifting."*

*"Disney always empowers me to be fun and light-hearted on a daily basis."*

On the flip side, brands that make Millennial Moms feel bad about themselves, as shown in these Millennials' comments below, reveal common tactics about unrealistic models with unrealistic bodies.

*"I absolutely hate fitness brands that market only to those that they feel fit their target demographic already. A company that is supposedly about fitness and health, and talks about helping people get in shape/live a healthier lifestyle that only utilizes size 0 – 2 models who look perfect makes me feel like a complete waste of their time and not worthy of their product."*

*"I don't exactly get a smile on my face when brands such as Victoria's Secret show only women who fit into a certain body type wearing their products."*

*"As far as a brand making me feel negative? I have yet to run into that issue, but if I do, I'll simply cut ties with that brand. I have no room for negativity in my life."*

*"Some clothing companies I think make most women, not just me, feel bad about themselves when they show women in bikinis with perfect bodies. Especially as mothers, not all of us can have that and it's not realistic to us."*

## #202 Millennial Moms have advice for brands.

Despite the diverse views of moms that greatly affect brand engagement strategies, a few consistent themes emerged when we asked moms for their best advice for marketers. I thought it would be beneficial to pull direct quotes from our research and share them with you.

There are several themes that emerged among many. First,

Millennial Moms are not unlike previous generations in their desire for products and services that save them money and time. Millennials, however, want brands to do more than talk *to* them. They want engagement, recognition and acknowledgment that they are important consumers, individually and as a cohort. A great many moms advised brands to keep it real, to pass on celebrity spokespersons and represent motherhood as it truly is for a Millennial. Finally, there are lots of words of advice regarding social media, an important platform for the conversation that's required to connect with Millennial Moms.

*"Connect on a personal level. Talk our language, which is primarily visual."*

*"Be real, believe in your product, educate."*

*"Respond to tweets and social media posts and listen."*

*"We don't want celebrities . . . we want people who are just like us."*

*"Create ads that engage moms on a level that says, 'We know you are busy and often multi-tasking.' Stop using ad campaigns that showcase all moms sitting around drinking coffee while their children play. Be realistic about the life of many working Millennial mothers."*

*"Connect!! Engage!! Talk to them."*

*"Know what we want — good products that help us save time."*

*"Target social media and blogs, that's where they are."*

*"Mail me a coupon or sample! 9x out of 10, I will buy it and give it a try."*

*"There are many local mom's groups in bigger cities. I am constantly amazed how strong of an influence word of mouth has in these groups. The moms in my groups ask for opinions and recommendations on EVERYTHING."*

*"Heavy social media presence, quick response via those outlets [i.e., don't create a page and rarely manage it]."*

*"Make sure you use technology and appeal to their family."*

*"Connect with them through social media."*

*"I would say be more vocal on social media, offer discounts and coupons and send mailers."*

*"Value what the moms bring to the table."*

*"Just reach out to people who are following you on your social media channels. Reach out over Twitter or Facebook, then follow up over email. Engage with us over Twitter and Facebook and talk to us, and get a feel for our interest in your products."*

*"Pay real people to give their opinions and have them reach out to other moms."*

*"Get real people to help advertise. I love real Mom (or real women) brand ambassadors' reviews when I'm shopping for clothing, nutrition, cars, etc."*

*"Show practical products and how they can make life easier. I like to see varieties of products, an easy way to shop."*

*"Photos and videos that can grab someone's attention are a plus!"*

*"Be authentic."*

# CONCLUSION

There you have it. My 202 facts to help you connect with Millennial Mothers. Applying even one of these nuggets of knowledge to your marketing plan could make a substantial difference in results. My advice is to start small. Determine the value proposition of your product, do a lot of social listening and see how you can align your brand in the conversations Millennial Moms are having about you, your product and the problem it solves for them.

Through these three easy steps, you will likely uncover a world of other marketing tactics. You'll discover which social media Mom Influencers are fans of your brand, who is already talking about your product and which Facebook groups are eager to find a solution your product offers. You are likely to find corporate partners who can expand your reach. Once you are ready to engage with Millennial Moms, select a platform or two that you are comfortable using and one that is relevant to your audience. Don't build out a communication plan for the next 12 months. You have to be more authentic than posting a whole lot of canned conversations. It's okay to have a communication calendar for your overall objectives each month, but make sure you're using social media to have a conversation with Millennial Moms. Keep in mind that it's called "social" media for a reason: you are meant to be socially engaged.

Finally, you have me in your court to help as well. If along the way you have questions, I'm just a tweet, post or phone call away. I'm happy to share my thoughts, suggestions or opinions on your strategy or tactics. You can find me at @momtalkradio, and (954) 943-2322.

Millennial Moms present a multibillion-dollar opportunity for brands that take the time to learn a little about what moves and motivates them. You've taken the first steps in understanding this large cohort of tech-savvy mothers and now it's time to begin. I wish you well as you connect with them, and I look forward to seeing your success in my #hashtag stream.

# NOTES

## The General Facts

1. US Census Bureau, "Millennials Outnumber Baby Boomers and Are Far More Diverse", Census Bureau Report, June 25, 2015, census.gov. http://www.census.gov/newsroom/press-releases/-2015/cb15-113.html

2. Teal, Theresa, "Millennial Moms In the US", Bard Advertising Blog, February, 2015. http://www.bardadvertising.com/blog/millennial-moms-in-the-u-s/

3. Ibid.

4. Pew Research Study; Social & Demographic Trends, "Millennials in Adulthood: Detached from Institutions, Networked with Friends,", March 2014, *PewResearch.org.*

5. Centers for Disease Control & Prevention, "Unmarried Childbearing", Jan. 22, 2015, *cdc.gov* http://www.cdc.gov/nchs/fastats/unmarried-child-bearing.htm

6. Pew Research Study; Social & Demographic Trends, "Millennials in Adulthood: Detached from Institutions, Networked with Friends", March 2014, *PewResearch.org.*

7. U.S. Department of Health and Human Services, "Trends in Teen Pregnancy and Child Bearing", 2013, *hhs.gov.* http://www.hhs.gov/ash/-oah/adolescent-health-topics/reproductive-health/teen-pregnancy/trends.html

8. US Chamber of Commerce Foundation, "The Millennial Generation Research Review", n.d., *USChamberFoundation.org.* http://www.uschamber- foundation.org/millennial-generation-research-review

9. The Nielsen Company, "Millennials – Breaking The Myths", page 16, 2014.

10. Durando, Jessica, "Why Nationwide aired upsetting Super Bowl ad", USA Today, Feb. 2, 2015, *USAToday.com.* http://www.usatoday.com/story/-money/2015/02/02/nationwide-insurance-superbowl-commer-cial/22734895/

11. Ibid.

12. "GoDaddy Issues an Apology for Their Super Bowl Commercial", Jan. 28, 2015, *Superbowl-commercials.org*. http://www.superbowl-commercials.org/34998.html

## Millennials as Moms

1. Dua, Tanya, "The mother of all generations: 5 things brands should know about millennial moms", May 13, 2015, *Digiday.com*

2. Baby Center Report, "Millennial Mom Report, 2014, *Babycenter.com* http://www.babycentersolutions.com/docs/BabyCenter_2014_CA_Millennial_Mom_Report.pdf

3. Wang, Wendy and Taylor, Paul, "For Millennials, Parenthoood Trumps Marriage", Pew Research Social & Demographic Trends, Mar. 9, 2011. http://www.pewsocialtrends.org/2011/03/09/for-millennials-parenthood-trumps-marriage/

4. Williams, Alex, "For Millennials, the End of the TV Viewing Party", New York Times, Nov., 7, 2014, *NYTimes.com*. http://www.nytimes.com/2014/-11/09/fashion/for-millennials-the-end-of-the-tv-viewing-party.html?_r=2

## Technology

1. Nanji, Ayaz, "How Different Generations Use Smartphones", July, 2014, *Marketingprofs.com*

2. Ibid.

3. Johnson, Lauren. "How Starbucks, Target are getting millennial mom marketing right", April 7, 2014, *Mobile Marketer.*

4. US Entertainment Consumer Report, "On-Demand Music Streamers By Age", 2013, *The Nielsen Company*

## Influence

1. Hoffman, Gretchen, "Where Fashion-Focused Millennials Find Inspiration", Nov., 18, 2013, *CMO.com* http://info.netbase.com/Millenials-Retail-Ebook.html?ls=Website&d=EBP-SocialChannelsInfluence-Millennials

## Work

1. Ramanan, Sai, "Why Does Every Tech Company Have a Ping-Pong Table?", October 25, 2014, *Quora.com.*

2. Valiente, Guillermo, "Serving the Millennial Generation", February, 2013, *Contactcenterpipeline.com*

## Finances

1. Robles, Maj. General Josue (Ret.), "Millennial Matters", USAA magazine, page 3, Fall 2014.

2. Data Points, AdWeek magazine, Aug., 11, 2014

## Shopping

1. Johnson, Lauren. "How Starbucks, Target are getting millennial mom marketing right", April 7, 2014, *Mobile Marketer.*

2. J. Walter Thompson report, "The Future of Payments and Currency," October 22, 2014, *jwt.com.* http://www.jwt.com/blog/consumer_ insights/jwts-the-future-of-payments-currency-trend-report-explores-new-ways-to-pay-and-rise-of-alternative-currencies/

3. "The Growth of Cause Marketing", Jan., 2014, *Causemarketing-forum.com.*

4. The Nielsen Company, "Millennials – Breaking The Myths", 2014

## Millennial Made

1. Phillips-Donaldson, Debbie, "Baby Boomers step aside; Millennials Now Own More Pets", April 1, 2015, *Petfoodindustry.com.* http://www.petfood-industry.com/articles/5049-baby-boomers-step-aside-millennials-now-ow n-more-pets

2. "Millennial Generation, Research Review", US Chamber of Commerce Foundation, n.d., *uschamberfoundation.org*

3. *Harwell, Drew,* "Marriott's new millennial-aimed hotel room: Stylish, cheap and smaller than 200 square feet", Jan. 21, 2015, *WashingtonPost.com.*

4. Anderson, Monica and Caumont, Andrea, "How Social Media is Reshaping News", Sept. 24, 2014, *PewResearch.org,*

## Family Life

1. Maycotte, H.O., "Millennials Are Driving The Sharing Economy — And So Is Big Data", May 5, 2015, *Forbes.com.* http://www.forbes.com/sites/-homaycotte/2015/05/05/millennials-are-driving-the-sharing-economy-and -so-is-big-data/

**Food**

1. "Millennial Target: Chipotle Has Fresh Appeal", Millennial Marketing Blog, 2015, *millennialmarketing.com.*

2. Jargon, Julie "McDonald's Facing Millennial Challenge", The Wall Street Journal Business, Aug., 24, 2014, *wsj.com.*

3. Fromm, Jeff, Lindell, Celeste and Decker, Lainie, "American Millennials: Deciphering the Enigma Generation", 2011, Barkley US.

# ACKNOWLEDGEMENTS

There may be only one name on the cover of this book but it is a collective effort of many. Some people spent hours and hours helping me while others don't even realize they contributed to the completion of *Millennial Moms*. Let me begin to express my gratitude.

Thank you to every person who had to hear me say, "I can't do it until my book is done." I know there were many, from the cashier at Publix to mom friends. I tried to keep the level of work I devoted to writing this book to myself but it wasn't always possible.

Only an insane person would try to write a book while earning her MBA from the University of Notre Dame. There. The truth about me is out in the open. I sometimes don't know how to say no to a good challenge and this was one of those times. I want to thank my MBA teammates Dustyn Arney, Steve Carollo and Ryan Cushing, who had my back on accounting equations and finance homework when I faced publisher deadlines. They are each successful professionals in industries far from Mom Marketing but each is also a fantastic Millennial Dad. I've filled their heads with more than they ever wanted to know about the buying behaviors of mothers. Thank you also to Julianna Giraldo, Bridig O'Connor, Lee Andreatta and Lainey Garcia and for all the encouragement during my weekends at Notre Dame. Go Irish!

My clients are the reason I work so hard to stay abreast of everything new in the Mom Market. I strive to be the best for you. Lori Lorenz, Leanne O'Regan, Amy Wells, Jen Cherry, Lois Lesley, Debbie Ann White, Maggie Riveria and Jennifer Labit, it is a privilege and joy to work with you. I love finding ways to raise the bar on marketing to mothers. To Noah Lomax, my expert Millennial marketer and client, thank you for all the lengthy and engaging discussions about your peer group. It's been energizing to strategize with such a brilliant young mind. Thank you for contributing your insights and expertise to *Millennial Moms*.

To my team at BSM Media — ElizaBeth Fincannon, Mary Donnellan, Laura Motsett, Shauna Lewis, Melanie Yerman, Natalie Zupo, Lauren Berger, Amy Sobel and Ellen Jacobs — I am lucky to have such an excellent team of creative women. They are dedicated to producing results for our clients and work hard to maintain relationships with over 10,000 highly influential moms around the globe. I know when I told them that *we* were going to write another book, they knew that it would mean long nights and weekends proofing but they never once blinked. Thank you, gang, for always bringing my ideas to life and, most importantly, thank you for banging out this book with me.

Thank you to Nancy Cleary, CEO of Wyatt-MacKenzie Publishing, who takes my books from concept to reality. She has been waiting two years for *Millennial Moms* and she finally has it. I want to credit Scott Hess, SVP of Human Intelligence for the media agency Spark, who coined the term "Post Generation" for the generation that follows the Millennials. I've never met Scott but I hope to one day, because I enjoy reading his insights.

There are lots of friends who don't get to see me as often as I would like because I am always writing. I look forward to sharing stories over a meal very soon. Thank you, Audrey Ring, Debbi Telli, Jennifer Calhoun, Jill Oman, Diego Rodriquez and Carter Auburn for your lifetime of support. To my special young entrepreneur friend Megan McGee: I hope your journey into business brings you much success. My thanks to Rebecca Levey, Nancy Friedman, Susan Pazera, Amy Hodges, Maria Ramos, Nicole Brady, Renee Ross, Desiree Miller and all the moms who I never have enough time with but support me constantly in business.

Thank you to my family for putting up with the stress that writing a book and earning an MBA can create in a home. I couldn't do anything I do without your inspiration and support. To Tim, my husband, thank you for your consistent support. Madison, Owen, Keenan and Morgan, I do everything for your benefit and you make the effort so worthwhile. And to my dad: I love you more than a daughter ever could love a father. You are the best.

# ABOUT THE AUTHOR

**Maria T. Bailey**

*Ad Age* calls her "One of the Must-Follow Women on Social Media" and credited her with creating the Marketing to Moms niche. Maria Bailey is an award-winning author, radio talk show personality, internationally known speaker and the foremost authority on marketing to moms. Her company, BSM Media is a full-service marketing and media firm that specializes in connecting brands with mothers. She has worked with over 300 brands across the globe including Disney, Wal-Mart, Kimberly Clark and Coca-Cola. She is the owner of MomTV.com, Blue-SuitMom.com, MomSelect.com and SmartMomSolutions.com

Maria helped to create successful programs such as *Huggies Mom Inspired, Disney Social Media Moms Celebration, Beaches Resorts Social Media On The Sand, HP Smart Moms* and the *Chick-fil-A's Mom Panel.* She was the marketing partner for the launch of Zhu Zhu Pets (2012 Toy of the Year), and founder of National Mom's Nite Out. She is a keynote speaker and media industry expert.

Maria is the author of seven books focused on marketing to moms. *Marketing to Moms: Getting Your Share of the Trillion Dollar Market* (Prima, 2002) is the first to examine the buying power of mothers and the most effective marketing initiatives. *Trillion Dollar Moms: Marketing to a New Generation of Mothers* (Dearborn, 2005) focuses on the emergence of Generation X and Generation Y moms and the comparison with Boomer Moms. In *Mom 3.0: Marketing with Today's Mothers by Leveraging New Media & Technology* (Wyatt-MacKenzie, 2008), Maria explores blogs, vlogs and social media. *Power Moms: The New Rules for Engaging Mom Influencers Who Drive Brand Choice* (Wyatt-MacKenzie, 2011) is a resource for marketers who want to identify the strongest mom influencers and offers suggestions for connecting with these powerful women.

*For the Love of Mom* (HCI, 2012) and *The Ultimate Mom Book* (HCI, 2010) are Maria's only non-marketing publications but nonetheless offer stories about everyday mothers.

With an audience that spans websites, blogs, YouTube channels, nationally syndicated radio and print publications, Maria reaches approximately 8 million moms each month. She is the host of Mom Talk Radio, the only nationally syndicated radio show for moms in America.

Maria has appeared on CNN, ESPN's Between the Lines, CNBC, WABC NY, ABC Channel 10 Miami, CBS New York, The Morning Show and many more. She has appeared in over 400 newspapers, magazines and online publications including *The Wall Street Journal, BusinessWeek, Entrepreneur, O Magazine, SELF, Fitness, MONEY* and more.

You can reach Maria Bailey at:
**Maria@BSMMedia.com**
or
**@Momtalkradio** on Twitter, Instagram, Pinterest or Periscope

# INDEX